God. Wakefield masterfully captures the heart of this life-transforming method and breaks it down in a way contemporary people can understand and put into practice. In fact, I believe this is the clearest and most practical application of Ignatius's *Spiritual Exercises* I've ever read. However, readers should be forewarned. In keeping with the spirit of Ignatius's exercises, this book will challenge them like few books they are likely to read. It's not for the casual reader or curiosity seeker. But for those who are hungry and ready for a life-changing encounter with the living God, I seriously doubt there is a more practical and more profound resource than this book."

Gregory A. Boyd, author, *Letters from a Skeptic* and *Seeing Is Believing*

"As a Jesuit for 62 years, I have been formed by the Exercises of Ignatius of Loyola, our principal founder. During 50 years of priesthood I have been privileged to direct them hundreds of times on every continent, often the entire Exercises of 30 days, and more often shorter adaptations. I rejoice, then, at the long-awaited publication of *Sacred Listening: Discovering the Spiritual Exercises of Ignatius Loyola*, adapted especially for Protestants, by James Wakefield. Not only does Wakefield interpret this short spiritual classic excellently, he admirably adapts them for devout Protestants who cherish the essentials of their great heritage. Only one who understands and loves the deep spiritual dimensions of this heritage could have written this book. It will be for its readers, I hope, a classic manual for spiritual growth in genuine mystical prayer. May its readership continue to grow."

Armand M. Nigro, S.J., professor emeritus, Gonzaga University

"James Wakefield has provided us with a remarkably helpful introduction to praying with the *Spiritual Exercises*, readable and eminently helpful, insightful and practical. Also notable: he builds on the best scholarship on the Exercises and makes it accessible to Christians of all traditions."

Gordon T. Smith, president, reSource Leadership International

SACRED LISTENING

DISCOVERING

THE SPIRITUAL EXERCISES

OF IGNATIUS LOYOLA

JAMES L. WAKEFIELD

BakerBooks
Grand Rapids, Michigan

Derek — Wow! We are on a good journey together. Thanks for the friendship. James 1/11/08

© 2006 by James L. Wakefield

Published by Baker Books
a division of Baker Publishing Group
P.O. Box 6287, Grand Rapids, MI 49516-6287
www.bakerbooks.com

Printed in the United States of America

Library of Congress Cataloging-in-Publication Data
Wakefield, James L., 1954–
    Sacred listening : discovering the Spiritual exercises of Ignatius Loyola / James L. Wakefield.
        p.   cm.
    Includes bibliographical references (p.   ) and index.
    ISBN 10: 0-8010-6614-X (pbk.)
    ISBN 978-0-8010-6614-6 (pbk.)
    1. Spiritual life. 2. Spiritual exercises. 3. Ignatius, of Loyola, Saint, 1491–1556. Exercitia spiritualia. I. Ignatius, of Loyola, Saint, 1491–1556. Exercitia spiritualia. II. Title.
    BV4501.3.W347 2006
    248.3—dc22   2006008652

CONTENTS

5

Contents

PREFACE

A Testimony of Ongoing Conversion

I have always been suspicious of religion. Cynicism comes too easily to me. Although I was raised in a staunch Mormon family, I became an atheist as an early teenager. Tragic events in my family led me to seek some spiritual reality at age nineteen, and I became a Christian. After this conversion in 1973, I finished a degree in world religions and went to seminary. My life was reasonably tranquil in September of 1984. I was a pastor in my second congregation. I helped start a theological seminary, and I was experiencing substantial professional satisfaction. My mother (now an Episcopalian) asked if I would like to do the *Spiritual Exercises* of Ignatius Loyola with a group that she was directing as part of a master's project under Father John Sheets, S.J., at Creighton University. I knew very little about the *Spiritual Exercises*, but I knew that they were Roman Catholic. I also remembered an article on "spirituality" in *Discipleship Journal* (a decidedly Protestant publication) reporting that the *Spiritual Exercises* were "a great spiritual classic."[1] I finally agreed to be part of her project because I wanted to protect her from "Roman Catholic mysticism." The cynic within complained bitterly!

In retrospect, I am greatly pleased the cynic lost. My experience of the *Spiritual Exercises* has been life changing. I found myself somewhat ruefully saying I felt I had been born again — again. Thinking back over the past twenty years, I can report four lasting benefits.

First, my relationship with the Lord is much more personal than it had been, and I pray often as I move through each day.

Second, I rediscovered that the Gospels are stories and that they communicate powerfully as such. Somewhere, in the midst of academia, the Gospels had become merely a source for teaching and preaching. Now they are filled with wonder and mystery.

Third, in the *Spiritual Exercises* I learned a descriptive code of rules for "discerning spirits." As commonsense as these rules now seem to me, I had never made the very practical connections Ignatius points out for us. These have become foundational in my Christian walk, in my counseling, and in my teaching and preaching.

Finally, the *Spiritual Exercises* called me to a more physical discipleship and to a profound freedom with Christ. As I learned to pray with my imagination and my five senses, I discovered a deep desire to experience God's greater glory in this wonderful and broken world.

A Brief History of *Sacred Listening*

As I finished the *Spiritual Exercises* in the spring of 1985, I began to consider how I might adapt them for use by others who do not have access to a spiritual director. My director used a guidebook published by John A. Veltri, S.J., and based the meditations on a very literal translation of the *Spiritual Exercises*.[2] My experience with these guides was excellent, and yet the material as written posed many problems as I considered giving the *Spiritual Exercises* to leaders in Protestant congregations. I began reworking and paraphrasing the *Spiritual Exercises* so that they could be used by Protestant Christians with minimal supervision from a trained spiritual director. This means I have had to wrestle with the dynamics of the *Exercises* in sufficient depth to anticipate most of the common stumbling blocks. I have made many changes as I continue to listen and to train other listeners, with encouraging results.[3] I have had many collaborators, and it is only right to recognize them here.

I field-tested my first revision with congregational leaders at Sonrise Baptist Church in West Jordan, Utah, in the summer of 1985 stretching into spring of 1986. These eleven adults were patient with many problems, and I learned much from them and their struggles. After I shared some of these adventures at a meeting for local clergy, the Reverend Tom Ashbrook asked me to train his leadership team at Good Shepherd Lutheran Church in Sandy, Utah. These twenty-seven adults offered many helpful comments between October 1986 and April 1987. A group of mental health workers heard about these adventurous Lutherans and asked me to guide them into contemplative prayer beginning in September 1987 stretching through April 1988. This group, coordinated by Dr. Linda Webster, allowed me an excellent opportunity to discuss many of the difficulties that might be encountered as persons pray with these Exercises.

I used parts of our original *Sacred Listening* manual in many of the classes I taught at the Utah Institute for Biblical Studies over the next decade.[4] Tom Ashbrook and I self-published the manual in 1986 at Good Shepherd. I revised the manual again in 1990 and mailed it to many of the authorities I most respected. Several of these authors and spiritual directors offered suggestions and encouragement, prompting another revision in 1992. Tom had moved to a new congregation, and so this version was published by Our Savior's Lutheran Church in Lake Oswego, Oregon. Minor revisions occurred when we used the manual with various groups: for a graduate seminar on spiritual direction at Salt Lake Theological Seminary in 1999; for undergraduate courses on Christian discipleship at Marquette University in 2001 and 2002; with two more large groups at Good Shepherd Lutheran Church; and for a semester-long course at Salt Lake Theological Seminary during the 2005 spring term. My students and congregants have offered some wonderful insights, and I have made a few adjustments yet again.

Tom Ashbrook and I have become lifelong friends and collaborators. He continues to use *Sacred Listening* and has made many helpful suggestions. My mother, Bonnie Joia Roddy, was ordained an Episcopal priest. She has used *Sacred Listening* since 1987 with many disciples and has also made many helpful suggestions. I owe profound debts to Ignatius, to several Jesuits, and to many more generous people who have written to give me suggestions and encouragement.[5] I am also grateful to Bonnie Julian, Margaret Montreuil, and Dr. Jeannette A. Bakke. All three of these spiritual directors have read the manuscript at various stages and have encouraged me to persevere. Ken Mulholland, Tom McClenahan, and David Rowe of Salt Lake Theological Seminary are part of the brain trust that has stimulated me for more than two decades. I hope and pray that *Sacred Listening* will help many Christians acquire a taste for the greater glory of God in the midst of everyday life.

Finally, it is my privilege to thank and to recognize the editorial skills of Chad Allen and Barb Barnes at Baker Books. They have made many suggestions, helped me see dozens of blind spots, and helped this become a more user-friendly book.

James Wakefield
November 1, 2005

PART ONE

INSTRUCTIONS FOR SACRED LISTENING

The days are surely coming, says the LORD, when I will make a new covenant with the house of Israel and the house of Judah. It will not be like the covenant that I made with their ancestors when I took them by the hand to bring them out of the land of Egypt—a covenant that they broke, though I was their husband, says the LORD. But this is the covenant that I will make with the house of Israel after those days, says the LORD: I will put my law within them, and I will write it on their hearts; and I will be their God, and they shall be my people. No longer shall they teach one another, or say to each other, "Know the LORD," for they shall all know me, from the least of them to the greatest, says the LORD; for I will forgive their iniquity, and remember their sin no more.

Jeremiah 31:31–34 NRSV

An Introduction
to the
Spiritual Exercises

What Are the *Spiritual Exercises*?

Over the past several years, I have asked many people what they know of the *Spiritual Exercises* of Ignatius of Loyola. Most Roman Catholics who know anything about them seem to think they are very difficult and only for those who are making religious vows. Many Protestants have not heard of them, and those who have consider them to be very Roman Catholic. In fact, *the* Spiritual Exercises *are an invitation to renew and deepen our relationship with Christ*. They are not a call to intellectual gymnastics, and they do not teach a set of theological propositions. The *Spiritual Exercises* are primarily a series of meditations on the Gospels that help us clarify and deepen our commitments to Jesus Christ. Specifically, in the

Spiritual Exercises we are encouraged to seek, recognize, and choose the greater glory of the kingdom of God in all things. A brief sketch of Ignatius's biography will help us understand what the *Spiritual Exercises* are and where they came from.

Ignatius was born in the Loyola family castle about 1491 in a Basque province in northern Spain.[1] As the youngest of perhaps a dozen children, he had no prospect of an inheritance, and his father sent him at about age fifteen, after minimal education, to serve as a page in the Spanish court. Ignatius was trained as a courtier and served in the retinue of the chief treasurer. When his patron died in 1517, he joined the military and eventually found himself defending a castle in Pamplona, Spain, against French attackers. On May 20, 1521, Ignatius was struck by a cannonball that broke one leg and badly damaged the other. In deference to his valor, the French set the bones in his legs and escorted him back to the Loyola family castle.

After weeks of convalescence, he had his legs rebroken and set again so he would look better in hosiery when he danced at the court. Reading became his principal pastime as he recuperated. Although accustomed to chivalrous tales, their short supply in the family castle led him finally to read Ludolph of Saxony's *Life of Christ* and the lives of the saints found in Jacopo de Voragine's *The Golden Legend*.[2] He began to imagine himself imitating the saints and soon noticed that he felt happy when he thought about spiritual things. Conversely, he felt sad when he gave his thoughts to worldly affairs. He came to understand these feelings as the effects of good and evil spirits, who influenced him as he gave himself to spiritual or worldly reading.[3] His conversion progressed quickly, and by September 1521 he began to copy and abridge the more important items of the life of Christ and the saints to carry with him on a future pilgrimage to Jerusalem. Leaving the family castle in late February 1522, he purposed not only to imitate the saints but to surpass their piety with acts of more severe penance.[4]

He arrived at the abbey in Montserrat on March 21, 1522. The priest assigned him three days of meditations on his past in preparation for confession.[5] Ignatius made his confession, left his armor at a shrine, and gave his fine clothes to a poor man. Taking the rough clothes of a pilgrim, he journeyed to Manresa and begged alms for support while he gave himself to prayer and study. Over the next many months, God humbled him through a series of visions and difficult trials. Ignatius eventually penned the majority of his *Spiritual Exercises* at Manresa as he reflected on his own conversion and growth in the spiritual life in dialogue with Thomas à Kempis's *Imitation of Christ* and Ludolph of Saxony's *Life of Christ*.[6]

Ignatius had further adventures in Jerusalem, Salamanca, and Barcelona, and finally took his master of arts in theology at the University of Paris in 1535. It was here that he began to train others with the *Spiritual Exercises*. These Exercises had a profound effect, and his early associates became so zealous for a relationship with Christ that Ignatius and his companions were accused of being Lutherans in disguise.[7] By the time they founded the Society of Jesus in 1540, the *Spiritual Exercises* were well known for promoting Christian faith and holiness. Over the next century these Jesuits showed their commitment to Christ by sending missionaries around the world.[8]

Since very early in the Society of Jesus's history, the *Spiritual Exercises* have been given in thirty-day silent retreats by a trained spiritual director.[9] The disciple and director meet on a daily basis and adjust the meditations to fit the issues raised during the disciple's five one-hour periods of prayer. The *Spiritual Exercises* often facilitate an intense examination of the disciple's motives for ministry, and so prove to be an excellent tool for making vocational choices.[10]

Even in Ignatius's day, the Jesuits recognized that some laypeople would profit greatly by doing or "making" the *Spiritual Exercises*, and so a plan was devised for these disciples to pray for about an hour and a half a day and meet weekly with their director over thirty weeks. This plan was called the Nineteenth Annotation because it was the nineteenth of twenty preliminary notes given to directors. In recent years, the *Spiritual Exercises* have been adapted to comprise three-, eight-, and twelve-day retreats.[11] These retreats are sometimes individually directed and sometimes preached (meaning directions for subsequent prayer are shared as sermons), and the individuals are given time to contemplate the Gospel passages. It is primarily through these shorter retreats that the public is becoming aware of the *Spiritual Exercises*.

Over the years, use of the Exercises has taken an almost endless variety of forms. Some use the Exercises as a personal devotional, while others use them as a resource to inform other methods of spiritual growth. Some of the daily assignments have been used in the context of corporate worship. Many more practices are in use, and still others are sure to emerge.

Sacred Listening is an adaptation of the *Spiritual Exercises of Ignatius Loyola* for contemporary people with little or no formal training in spiritual disciplines. This adaptation accommodates a regular work schedule, highlights the scriptural inferences of the original Exercises, incorporates small revisions to avoid unnecessarily alienating Protestants, and allows for use with small groups. Undertaking the Exercises without a companion—which is strongly discouraged—will be discussed at length in chapter 2. Ideally, pastors, spiritual directors, mentors, and small group leaders will encourage the use of *Sacred Listening* to introduce spiritually hungry people to contemplative prayer. The initial commitment is sixty to ninety minutes each day for the eight weeks of the first movement.[12] The full exercises of *Sacred Listening* take at least twenty-four weeks.

Spiritual Exercises for Protestants

There is some evidence that the first generation of Jesuits shared the *Spiritual Exercises* with Protestants.[13] One may well ask, why would Protestants want anything to do with what could be called "Jesuit boot camp"? Ignatius invites us into the story of Jesus and calls us to be transformed by our participation in the story. With our imagination and reason, with our five bodily senses, and especially with our emotions, we become secondhand witnesses of the events of Scripture. Ignatius supplements these meditations on the Gospels with certain parables and themes that help us clarify our feelings. We are called to desire God above all things, and we are taught to love our neighbors sacrificially. Secure in God's love for us, we learn to experience God's peace in every situation.

Sacred Listening shapes the Exercises as a school for discipleship and prayer.[14] Because the *Spiritual Exercises* were originally given in thirty days, the four major sections became known as the "four weeks," and this terminology is sometimes used even when giving the thirty-week version. To avoid confusion in *Sacred Listening*, I identify each Ignatian week as a "movement," for as in a fine symphony, we are carried by many smaller sections toward a specific response.

The next chapter discusses in more detail an ideal schedule for beginning the Exercises, and sample schedules are provided in Using *Sacred Listening* with Groups (pp. 186–87).

First Movement

The first Ignatian movement leads disciples to discover the necessity for God's unmerited forgiveness and mercy. This discovery is encouraged as disciples reflect on the goodness of God as seen in creation and Scripture, consider a basic statement that defines the purpose of life, and then meditate on their own sin history and its likely results. This is not meant to be depressing or morbid but has its purpose in creating a space within us that the Lord can fill. In *Sacred Listening* this movement is covered in eight units, each comprising seven days.[15]

17

The first unit focuses on God's goodness and is meant to introduce us to contemplative prayer. Three units are spent exploring our experience of God's love in the context of good times, hard times, and rebellious times. In the fifth unit, we compare the Principle and Foudation—a basic statement that defines the purpose of life—to the attitudes and actions of the apostle Paul as seen in Philippians. The last three units are spent reflecting on the consequences of sin. At strategic times we are asked to meditate on six intuitive Rules for Discernment that help us understand some of the causes and feelings underlying our choice of given actions.[16] Ignatius cautioned us that the material following unit 8 is not useful—and may even be harmful—to some people.[17] Therefore, in a long comment after unit 8, disciples are encouraged to count the cost of moving into the second movement.

Second Movement

The second Ignatian movement leads us to an appreciation of the humanity of Christ and by this to an identification with his goals, values, and methods.[18] By imaginatively contemplating scenes in the four Gospels, disciples are led to see the comprehensive goodwill of Jesus toward those who will accept his invitation to "come and follow me." In counterpoint to these meditations on the Gospels, Ignatius developed four of his own parables. These were drawn from his own culture and seek to illumine the call of Christ, to contrast Jesus's tactics with the strategies of the evil one, and to exemplify the responses of Jesus's disciples.[19]

These Exercises are extremely challenging because they lead us to question our commitment to Christ in very practical terms. Specifically, they confront us with our willingness to obey Christ in all things—especially in our pursuit of honor and riches. This movement occupies ten units. Seven more rules for discerning the causes of various feelings and decisions are assigned, helping us confront our value systems and to desire the Lord and his kingdom more and evermore.[20]

Third Movement

The third Ignatian movement calls disciples to contemplate the obedience and suffering of Christ—to appreciate the price of redemption and so count the cost of our discipleship. Disciples are asked to witness the suffering of Jesus through a series of imaginative role plays and meditations on the passion of Christ. In the present version, two units focus on this theme. The brevity of this third movement is required by its intensity, particularly when coordinated with the weeks before Easter.

Fourth Movement

The last movement leads us to strengthen our attachment to Christ. It begins tenuously, as we are asked to wrestle with the improbability of the resurrection. The discovery of a new and profound joy—the reality of the resurrection—draws us to ask, "How can I live before so great a King?" Ignatius supplied a beautiful prayer that summarizes our response. *Sacred Listening* provides four units within this movement that encourage us to strengthen our attachment to Christ. The fourth movement lasts as long as Jesus is Lord, and so *Sacred Listening* is just one beginning or step forward in deepening our spiritual life.

A Brief Outline of *Sacred Listening*

This chapter has introduced the *Spiritual Exercises* and their presentation in *Sacred Listening*. Reviewing the material in the next several chapters is essential before beginning the Exercises. Chapter 2 explains how to do or "make" the Exercises. Chapter 3 suggests a simple and helpful method of journaling. Chapter 4 gives some very brief instructions for listeners. The daily assignments are given in part 2.[21] The Rules for Discernment and Ignatian Parables are collected in a separate chapter called Ignatian Resources, followed by a summary chart and instructions for using *Sacred Listening* with groups. A glossary of terms is provided for quick reference. The book ends with a brief bibliography and suggested reading.

2

MAKING THESE
EXERCISES

SPIRITUAL GROWTH IS beyond all things a gift in and from the Holy Spirit. Apart from this Helper, all spiritual exercises are deadening. As you begin, ask the Holy Spirit to use this experience for your spiritual growth.

Your Goal in Making These Exercises

Your goal in making these Exercises is to grow in responsive spiritual freedom.[1] We seek freedom from our past, and we seek freedom from present constraints on our loving response to God. All spiritual exercises can be made on a superficial level in which the assignments become just nice little Bible studies or times of reflection. Beyond the superficialities of popular religion lies a path to deeper spirituality, in which you are called always to *live for the greater glory of God*. These Exercises will introduce you to a road on which you can discuss the process and substance of your life with your Lord.[2] The journey is lifelong. You should expect to finish these assignments only in preparation for continuing the Christian journey.

Reading Scripture with Our Lives

Sacred Listening invites you to learn to read the Bible in a different way. Because we hope to encounter God, we practice a form of sacred listening known as the *lectio divina*. Eugene Peterson helps us understand its importance and potential:

> *Lectio divina* is not a methodical technique for reading the Bible. It is a cultivated, developed habit of *living* the text in Jesus's name. This is the way, the *only* way that the Holy Scriptures become formative in the Christian church and become salt and leaven in the world.[3]

Sacred Listening uses a particular and extended application of the *lectio divina*. There are four parts to our sacred listening with Holy Scripture:

In the *lectio*, we read the text slowly, out loud if possible, and then sit in silence for several minutes. Many of the daily assignments in *Sacred Listening* instruct you to repeat this a few times before you are moved to meditate on the text. For the sake of simplicity and space, the daily assignments give the *lectio* reading assignment as part of the *meditatio*.

In the *meditatio*, we consider the text with our imagination and heart. Many of the daily assignments in *Sacred Listening* encourage you to *witness* a scene by taking a particular point of view or role in your imagination. Sometimes you are asked to sit in silence with the scene until you are moved to speak about it with the Lord.

In the *oratio*, we discuss the text and our response with the Lord. The daily assignments are intentionally nondirective here, because you will learn to follow the Holy Spirit as you ask for Jesus's help, correction, and guidance in living consistently with his will in your lifelong contemplation of the text.

The *contemplatio* is the lifelong experience of discovering how the text shapes us within our communities and within the kingdom of God. Section 2 of your journal (described in chapter 3) is meant to help you capture your ongoing contemplative experience and encourage joyful obedience to your Lord.

Using Your Imagination

Many of the daily assignments in *Sacred Listening* ask you to use your imagination. Some sincere people find this difficult because the majority of biblical texts about the imaginations, inclinations, or thoughts of our hearts are warnings against an evil intent and content. When we human beings initiate any process toward God, it goes badly for us. There is no exception for our imaginations. However, we might also ask, is all use of the imagination evil or idolatrous?[4] What if we are responding to God's initiative?

A few biblical texts encourage a responsive use of our thoughts and imagination. Philippians 4:8 commands us, "Whatever is true, whatever is noble, whatever is right, whatever is pure, whatever is lovely, whatever is admirable—if anything is excellent or praiseworthy—think about such things" (NIV). And Paul seems to encourage use of our imagination in response to God's grace in Ephesians 3:20–21.

While it might be tempting to claim that even mental images of Jesus are idolatrous, this does not square with the intent of the writers of our four Gospels. I offer as evidence this excerpt from "Notes on the Translation of the Greek Tenses" in the *New American Standard Bible.*

> In regard to the use of the historic present, the Board recognized that in some contexts the present tense seems more unexpected and unjustified to the English reader than the past tense would have been. But Greek authors frequently used the present tense for the sake of heightened vividness, thereby *transporting their readers in imagination to the actual scene at the time of occurrence.* However the Board felt that it would be wise to change these historic presents into English past tenses. Therefore verbs marked with an asterisk (*) represent historical presents in the Greek which have been translated with an English past tense in order to conform to modern usage.[5]

The italicized phrase emphasizes the Gospel writers' desire for readers and hearers to have a vivid experience of these stories about Jesus. They want us to see them as though we are *witnessing* the actual scene. It is one of the great tragedies of our age that we have allowed fear and the misuse of imagination to keep us from an experience of Jesus in and through the text of the Bible.[6]

Journaling

Keeping a spiritual journal is an important part of making the Exercises. For many, the journal we keep as part of the daily assignments becomes a treasured artifact to which we will refer again and again throughout our lives. The next chapter will explain in detail how to keep a journal while making the Exercises.

The Role of Listening

Crucial to making these Exercises is the process of *listening.* Ignatius's own listening led to the development of these

Exercises. And the person making them, commonly referred to as "the disciple" or "the Lord's disciple," will need to focus closely on listening to the Holy Spirit throughout the process, hence the title *Sacred Listening*.

Another way listening plays a role in these Exercises is through *listeners*. A listener is one who serves as a companion and listens to the disciple weekly for the duration of time a disciple makes the Exercises. The first and foremost role of a listener is quite simple: to listen. Other roles a listener plays include reflecting back to the disciple what the disciple has said, giving suggestions or second opinions when asked, and encouraging the disciple when things get tough. Chapter 4 provides more detailed instructions for listeners.

It is important to note that the Holy Spirit is the disciple's *first* listener and spiritual director. Second and third listeners are human companions with whom the disciple shares what it has been like to do the daily assignments. The general assumption of this book is that each individual on a listening team (of either two or three) is both a disciple (i.e., making the Exercises) and a listener for his or her companion(s). Although it is conceivable that a mature Christian could serve as a listener with little experience of the Exercises, this would be awkward at best. Ideally, your listener has either made the Exercises previously or is making them as a member of your listening team.

The Safety of Community

I anticipate many will use *Sacred Listening* in the context of an established program for spiritual formation or discipleship. An appendix provides guidelines for use by groups of more than three. Some will use it without human companions. Because the Exercises call us to such deep levels of reflection, there is some danger in making them without human companions. The danger varies to the degree that one has a sound knowledge of Scripture and accepted Christian practice. Few of us are so well balanced that we would not profit from the insight of other mature Christians. Ideally, your pastor would agree to make the Exercises with you and serve as a listener.[7] If he or she cannot, ask your pastor to refer one or two other mature and compassionate Christians to make the Exercises with you.

My own recommendation is for listening teams of three, especially if God is calling you to do these Exercises apart from an established program. Very often we find that our sense of accountability is heightened by the presence of a third person. A third person also allows mixed-gender teams and minimizes the risks of romantic entanglement. A third person can help limit an influential person's need to teach or redirect the listening process for his or her own purposes. And most important, a third person can be a valuable prayer partner as the Exercises challenge us with some difficult ideas about ourselves.

On the days you meet with your listener(s) you are asked to prepare by reviewing your journal. It is very important that you review carefully. Enter this review in your journal and, if possible, make a copy of your review to give your listener(s). These review days are critical to good progress in noticing how God is working in your life.[8]

Choosing Listeners

In addition to asking for your pastor's recommendations, carefully consider the qualities desirable in those who will make these Exercises with you. *Pray about whom to ask to be your listening partner(s) in these exercises.* You will meet weekly for many weeks, and the friendships established here may last a lifetime.

1. Listeners should be able to function within the lines of established authority.

2. Listeners should be able to listen and resist the need to teach or chat.
3. Listeners should have a thorough knowledge of Scripture and accepted Christian practice. Ideally, one listener will have already completed the *Spiritual Exercises* in some form and have some skill in discerning the movements and experiences of those making these Exercises. This is not essential but very helpful.
4. Listeners should have a deep love relationship with the Lord, as they may be challenged greatly by your experience.
5. Listeners must be willing to keep in strict confidence the content of your journal and prayer time, and agree to obtain your permission before discussing a confidence with a trusted leader for your benefit.
6. Experience has taught us that your listeners should not initially be too close an associate nor too intimate a friend. In the first case, your relationship may become quite strained during the Exercises. In the second case, your friendship may blind them to your needs or prejudice them against some aspect of your experience.
7. Listeners should be faithful in prayer, as you will need this additional support at several points in these Exercises.

Discipline Yourself

In field-testing these Exercises, one observation has proved itself time and time again. If you are consistent and seriously desire to know Christ better, these Exercises will encourage you to deepen your relationship with Jesus far beyond what you even now expect. No program of spiritual growth will succeed if it is not entered into with desire for greater intimacy with God. One purpose should motivate you: to know Christ better and so love him more. And yet, few disciples desire deep intimacy with the one described in Hebrews 12:29 as "a consuming fire," even if this consumption is for their own good.

Your emotions may change in many ways while making these Exercises. You may experience times of depression, during which you may hope merely to survive. You will have times of great joy and comfort during which you may think no exercise is difficult and no cost is too severe. Consistency is needed, not so much in motive as in committed time. If we are to become intimate, we must spend time with our Lord. This can be costly. Plan to spend at least an hour a day, and plan an extra hour or so on the days you meet with your listener(s). It may help to recall that few of us watched the clock during our adolescent infatuations. A genuine and consuming love can scarcely imagine too much time with our beloved.

These exercises are not for everybody. Consider the cost seriously before you begin. Several of those we have listened to have been half-hearted in their desire to pray. The results have been very discouraging. Almost always they drop out before the end of unit 8. They feel like failures and are less likely to attempt a serious program of prayer again.

Be Flexible and Follow the Holy Spirit

Some disciples find at times during these Exercises they have desired to pray differently than assigned.[9] In some cases this is not good because they are seeking to avoid a difficult confrontation with Christ. But often, because they are unique individuals who are becoming more sensitive to the Holy Spirit, their intuition to pray by approaching the text in a different manner from what is suggested has been rewarded by a rich time of communion with their Lord. At times they have even been called to a different text—often repeating a previous meditation—and by their obedience have experienced much encouragement.

Solid reason should be sought for each departure from the assigned text and method of prayer. Note your reasons for changing as part of the basic data in your journal for that period of reflection (chapter 3 discusses keeping a journal in detail). Discuss this with your listener(s). You are responsible to your Lord for these choices and encouraged to follow the Spirit's direction. After all, your goal is to draw closer to Christ and to enjoy his instruction.

Confronting Resistance

As we come closer to Christ, who is the Light of the World, we will suspect, and then discover, a great deal of darkness within our own souls. This is universally the experience of serious disciples and can be seen in the life of the apostle Paul. Consider this assessment by J. I. Packer:

> It looks as if Paul himself, as he advanced in years, and presumably in holiness, too, grew downward into an increasingly vivid and humbling sense of his own unworthiness; for whereas in 1 Corinthians (c. 54 AD) he called himself the very least of the apostles and in Ephesians (c. 61 AD) the very least of all the saints, in 1 Timothy (c. 65 AD) he describes himself as the foremost of sinners (see 1 Cor. 15:9; Eph. 3:8; 1 Tim. 1:15).[10]

At the outset we admit the courage it takes to truly look at the depth of our own depravity is beyond us. We embark on a perilous course that at once threatens and calls us. We are like the demonized man in Mark 5:1–20 who rushes up to Jesus and then pleads with him not to torment him.[11]

If you do not truly desire a deeper relationship with Christ, then you may become fixated in, or sometimes even regress in, your spiritual growth. As you make these Exercises, you may be led by the Holy Spirit to examine some dark and terrible things. It is quite natural to fear—and therefore to resist—these discoveries. One sign that you are resistant is that you are only "doing little Bible studies" and are not discussing them with the Lord. A second sign of resistance is that your prayer becomes dry and forced. During these times you are tempted to quit the whole enterprise. You must not, for the dangers and rewards are too great. The discovery of these dark secrets is in fact a cause for joy, for as you admit them, you can be freed from their dead weight.[12] The Exercises thus call us to a deep experience of the love and forgiveness which Christ offers us. Whether you are confronted with lust, pride, deceit, or rebellion, you can be confident that Jesus already knows your depths and will deliver you from these inner terrors.

Sometimes you may be afraid to report your struggles to your listener(s). You are not required to share everything. Pray, and choose wisely before you burden them with something they cannot deal with. Your choice is respected. But remember that confession is one of the surest steps to changing your behavior.[13] Your listener(s) should not make suggestions for change unless you ask for advice. But let them pray for and with you on these difficult matters.

Failure to confront these areas of resistance may stifle your relationship with Christ. God gives abundant grace—the empowering presence of the Holy Spirit is really with you—as you face these difficulties.[14] You are called by Christ to trust him even here.

Prolonged Dryness

Not all dry periods indicate that you are resistant. At various times in your walk with Jesus, it will appear that he has withdrawn from you. In these times you may be tempted to put unhelpful pressure on yourself to restore the vigor of the relationship. In the course of these Exercises you will consider why these times come and how you should respond. Hindsight may reveal these deserts are the most valuable time of your prayer. As in all of your prayers, you are called to wait patiently for God's purpose to be made clear.

Rules for Discernment and Ignatian Parables

In these Exercises you will be guided by a series of intuitive Rules for Discernment. These rules are observations about the way things usually happen. They are more descriptive than prescriptive.[15] The rules are introduced at strategic moments within these Exercises. You may at first find some of them confusing or difficult, but rest assured that these rules make more sense as you mature, and so you should pray for understanding and persevere in your meditations. You will discover their value intuitively as you use them.

Four Ignatian parables are introduced at opportune moments in the second movement. These were drawn from Ignatius's experience of his culture and help us understand more about the call of God in our lives.

The Rules for Discernment and the Ignatian parables are collected in a separate chapter at the end of the book for the sake of convenient reference.

The Value of Repetition

The Exercises make a calculated use of repetition. Our goal is not to impress God with our many words but to enter more deeply into an experience of his love. As you repeat a meditation, you will be tempted to think, *I have already done this.* Such thoughts could rob you of the great gift brought by repetition—growing simplicity and genuineness in your response to God. Let me illustrate: Recall the first time you confessed deep love for another person. Remember the forethought, the agony of how you planned your words. As your relationship deepened, and you made this confession more often, the process became much simpler and much more

31

genuine. Deep love allows both quiet and spontaneity. Deep prayer does too. Your attitude in making the assigned repetitions should be that of calm anticipation. Nothing dramatic has to happen.

Theme and Grace

Each seven-day unit focuses on a specific "theme." Often you will find that an assigned meditation captivates your attention for more than twenty-four hours. Do not rush the Holy Spirit! Do not be discouraged. Take the time needed to discuss it with your Lord. At the same time, remember that you will be repeating many of the assignments and so should avoid any intellectual trap of trying to exhaust each theme or text.

When you take longer than a day on a given meditation, you will fall behind for the scheduled weekly review with your listener(s). Several things can be done. Time permitting, you may do two meditations on the same day. The danger here is in going through the motions as opposed to meditating on the text and discussing it with your Lord. Ideally, these times of prayer should be separated by several hours so that you have time to notice the gifts God offers you. The other alternatives are to postpone your meeting or to just discuss what you have done. This last alternative is the best. Real prayer cannot be rushed.

Each unit has a "grace" as well. If the theme focuses our head, then the grace focuses our heart. In this context, a grace is a gift that we seek from God. We cannot obtain it by ourselves. Ask for the grace, and receive it as a gift. *Receiving this gracious gift is in fact the goal of each unit.* Seek this gift not only in your prayer time but all day long. You will want to respond to God's love and presence by increasing your awareness of God's goodness. Very often, the Holy Spirit orchestrates the events of your life to provide you with experiences of God's goodness. You will want to be careful to notice and thank God for these gifts.

An Ideal Schedule for Your *Sacred Listening* Exercises

If you are using *Sacred Listening* apart from an established program, you can begin at any time of the year. However, as explained below, it is most beneficial to begin the last week of September and complete the first movement by mid-December. This allows eleven weeks to complete the eight units. Pace yourself to allow for some free time around Thanksgiving and other events with your family and work. Use your extra days to deepen or repeat your meditations and seek additional insights about your walk with Christ as you develop the charts suggested in units 2, 3, 4, and 8.

How do you know which assignments to repeat? *Let the Holy Spirit guide you!* He may lead you to repeat meditations you had to hurry through. He may lead you to repeat meditations on passages of Scripture where you were challenged and blessed with a deeper sense of God's love. He may lead you to just rest in God's love or to use your time to do works of love and mercy, as in Ephesians 2:10. Enjoy being led by the Spirit of God.

Beginning the second movement in mid-December allows you to follow the Lord through his birth and life and complete the second movement two or three weeks before Easter. The date of our Easter celebration shifts from year to year: When Easter comes in late March, you will have fewer days to repeat meditations or take days off. When Easter falls late in April, you will have many days to repeat meditations, to do additional spiritual reading, or to take days off. (See pp. 186–87 for sample schedules.)

Allow two or three weeks for the third movement, and begin the fourth movement on Easter Sunday. Allow four to six weeks for the fourth movement, and then celebrate completing your first cycle of *Sacred Listening*.

3

How to Keep
a Spiritual Journal

W HEN ASKED TO describe an event at various inter-
vals after it occurs, we tend to give shorter accounts
with the passage of time. Our minds edit the details as more
recent events crowd our thinking. This is necessary for our
sanity and concentration.[1] But this editing function of our
minds can be a real hindrance to spiritual growth. Much of
our spiritual experience is so fleeting it escapes our conscious
memory altogether. Most of our experience is pushed aside by
more urgent matters and is lost to the conscious mind.

As we become serious about spiritual growth, we want to
examine even the most fleeting experience of God's love. This
can lead us to become so introspective that we have a difficult
time praying because we fear missing some detail of grace.
Jesuit Thomas Green points out that using a journal gives us
a place to analyze our experience apart from our prayers.[2] Few
tools will be more useful in teaching us to listen to God than

our spiritual journal. Consider this testimony from Gordon MacDonald:

> Slowly I began to realize that the journal was helping me come to grips with an enormous part of my inner person that I had never been fully honest about. No longer could fears and struggles remain inside without definition. They were surfaced and confronted. And I became aware, little by little, that *the Holy Spirit was directing many of the thoughts and insights as I wrote.* On paper, the Lord and I were carrying on a personal communion. He was helping me, in the words of David, to "search my heart." He was prodding me to put words to my fears, shapes to my doubts. And when I was candid about it, then there would often come out of Scripture, or out of the meditations of my heart, the reassurances, the rebukes, and the admonishments that I so badly needed. *But this began to happen only when the journal was employed. . . . When the journal opens, so does the ear of my heart.* If God is going to speak, I am ready to listen.[3]

Organizing Your Journal

The journal used in these Exercises is different from your schedule book, daily calendar, or diary. Its purpose is quite specific: to record your spiritual experiences in such a way that they can be appropriated and used in lasting growth. A three-ring binder and loose-leaf paper will allow you to expand it later with a minimum of hassle. I encourage daily entries of five sections each. Let me describe these to you, explain how they relate to your *lectio divina*, and give some examples.

Section 1: Note the Time and Location of Your Sacred Listening

At the start of each exercise period, write down your time and location, and any other significant aspect of your surroundings or physical condition. For example:

1. 7:00–7:55 a.m., in the living room, sitting on the couch, feeling quite hungry.

or

1. 4:30–5:30 p.m., in my office, feeling very tired after a long board meeting. I have a mild headache.

This discipline seems a little mundane, but it may yield valuable insights into your prayer time. The time and feelings prior to your meditation affect your prayers. Knowing that you had a headache as you approached a given text may explain at a later date why you had so much trouble praying at all.

Section 2: Review the Theme and Grace in Your Life (Contemplatio)

After this brief note on basic data, review your life since your last journal entry. How have you experienced the assigned theme and grace since your last exercise? While this is not meant to be a long period of reflection (five to ten minutes should be sufficient), this second section shows the practical results of your ongoing conversation with God. In this first example, the person is praying for the gift of humility, and he finds some freedom in repentance:

2. *Contemplatio*: Since yesterday, I have been aware how often I speak in defense of myself. The grace of humility calls me to leave this with Christ. Once I resisted defending myself, and it felt wonderful.

It may be very helpful to add specific comments about other events you are challenged by. In this second example, this person is reviewing how she has experienced the patience of Jesus:

2. *Contemplatio*: The patience of Christ has been very present in my thinking. I have twice resisted nagging my kids because I remembered his example. I did not resist arguing with my

spouse, and I feel the need to be more patient like our Lord. Christ, have mercy!

Frequently, while writing this second section you will recognize what God has been trying to get you to hear. This is because much of the work we do in meditation is just that—our work. This necessary effort prepares us to listen. Yet often we either listen too hard and so jump at every noisy thought, or we rush our prayer time so that we go away ready, willing, but empty. If we listen for God throughout the day, we will find that often he speaks to us while we are doing some routine task like doing the dishes or pulling weeds.[4] These experiences and insights into God's love for us should be recorded in section 2. For example:

2. *Contemplatio*: Yesterday I had a hard time focusing on John 15. I felt resentful that my life needs pruning. Tough metaphor. It was too cold to prune in the garden, but I cleaned the garage. My life is cluttered with lots of meaningless stuff. Maybe pruning isn't so bad? It's good for roses and fruit trees. And grapevines. Jesus is calling me closer—to abide with him. His call has sounded in me as I have seen my own emptiness. I hope he continues to call me closer.

This section helps you collect your thoughts and feelings and so brings to a close the previous day's meditation—in other words, the gist of your *contemplatio*.[5] It is *the most important section* of your journal. If you have time for nothing else, find time for at least this second section. In times of crisis, this may become the heart of your journal, calling you to be more aware and encouraging you to change and live in the grace you are asking for.

Section 3: Briefly Summarize Your Meditation (Meditatio)

After "collecting" yourself, do the assigned reading and meditation. *Pray first and then record what happened.* Ignatius suggested praying for an hour and then spending about fifteen minutes in review.[6] Summarize as much as you can in section 3 of your journal, but remember that your goal is to record your experience so it can be recalled later. Too brief an account may limit its usefulness. It will take some time to become comfortable in making this judgment. Allow yourself room to experiment. For example, while meditating on "the early trials of Jesus" and asking for gratitude that the Lord remained obedient and patient in suffering, one disciple wrote:

> 3. *Meditatio* on Luke 2:51–52; Hebrews 2:14–18: I imagine that Jesus also faced desolation in those years of early manhood. He didn't follow the crowd and do what all his friends were doing. I continue to struggle here. The temptations have been awesome since my divorce. I am so amazed and challenged by his perfect obedience! In my most honest moments, I wonder if I really want to be more like him. Lord, have mercy on me!
>
> Was Jesus ever impatient with the course his life was taking? Okay. I know Jesus was fully human and felt as we do. Did he hurt as much as I do? He must have! But yet feeling his Father's love kept him faithful? Why then do I feel so empty and unsatisfied?

The writer is in touch with a part of Jesus's life that many of us have given little thought to. You can see how powerful it is to make these brief notes and to reflect on our meditation as we go through the day.

Section 4: Speak about Your Feelings (Oratio)

The fourth part of your journal summarizes your prayer and focuses on your affective response—your emotions. Here you ask, "What do I feel in and because of my meditation?" You are not asking, "Do I like this?" but rather, "Am I more peaceful or more agitated as I seek this gift? Am I more trusting or distrustful of God's love as I follow Jesus in this meditation?"

The instructions for the *oratio* (e.g., "Discuss this with the Lord and thank him for the joy of following him") are often nondirective so as to allow you to follow the guidance of the Holy Spirit. You may be led to thank God for something other than the suggested thanksgiving.

You will most likely experience a broad range of emotions as you consider the assignments, as you focus on the theme, and as you seek God's gifts. Many persons have problems recognizing their feelings and try to squash those they do recognize. If you hope to be a mature spiritual person, you cannot hide from these feelings and your deeper emotions. You must seek to embrace them, know them, and grow in them. Consider Gordon T. Smith's summary of the role of feelings in Ignatius's thought:

> [Ignatius] was convinced that we could take God and ourselves seriously only if we learned to take emotion and affect seriously. Emotion and feeling were for Ignatius key indicators of the work of God in our lives, for by attending to emotional dispositions we are giving attention to the media of God's influence in our lives. Feelings are the information on which we focus when we seek the mind of the Lord.[7]

This Protestant voice parallels a Jesuit understanding that God can speak to us through our feelings.[8] A possible complication exists, however, because our feelings and deeper emotions are also part of *our* affective *oratio*—our nonverbal response to God. Our nonverbal responses are often critical in our human relationships. Are they any less important with God? As flesh-and-bone people, we respond to God with our bodies as well as with our minds. There is much to gain through paying attention to what we are saying with our bodies and feeling in our emotional responses. Here is how the same disciple (in section 3 above) summarizes his prayer. Notice it takes the form of a prayer and focuses on his feelings.

4. *Oratio*: Lord Jesus, I am impatient with myself, my ministry, MY timetable. I am chastised, and I ask for patience to wait, to remain faithful, until our loving Abba changes my life. I do feel empty and unsatisfied when I look at my life and hear the call to be obedient in suffering. Yes, I can be grateful that the Lord remained obedient and patient in suffering. But I feel guilty that I don't want to be patient. I can confess my impatience. I can even say the words, "I ask for patience to wait for your timing in all things." But my guts are churning and I feel hopeless some of the time. Maybe I need to change part of how I am praying? Lord Jesus, hear my whole prayer and grant me your peace.

This disciple is becoming aware of the difference between his verbal understanding and self-judgment and his deep need to trust God's love even more. Consider this experience from a disciple praying to learn humility from Christ:

4. *Oratio*: Lord, I'm afraid. Call it a lack of trust. I panic at false expectations. I'm at the place in my walk with you where I'm saying, "Lord, give me humility and the strength to stand the consequences." I need to simply ask, "Lord, give me the desire for humility." In reality, I ask for a desire for the desire for humility. Lord Jesus, please have your way with my life.

Her feelings are such that we can easily identify with them. In stating them, she allows herself to become much more aware and can begin to confront her lack of trust in this area. Over the next several weeks, she began to grow in trust. She looked back and rejoiced that she no longer felt the same way. Your growth will also be seen most clearly here. You will have good and bad days at prayer. But you will become consistently more attached to Christ and his opinion of you as you pray. As we are conformed to his image, we also gain his feelings about life and about ourselves. Section 4 encourages you to record this consonance of feeling with Christ, and we do not want to miss thanking God for such a gift.

Section 5: Your Summary

The fifth part of your journal summarizes your experience as you answer, "Where is God's grace in all this?" Specifically, we are looking to see how we have experienced the gracious gift we have asked for. Section 5 will help you prepare the review in day 7 of each unit. As you review your journal, focus on your feelings and experience (or lack of experience) of the grace you have sought from God.

This section also provides a good beginning for the *contemplatio* you will record in section 2 of the following day.

A Sample Journal Entry

Most people feel a little nervous during the first couple of weeks because they are not sure that they are journaling correctly. Individual journals will differ significantly, as seen in the previous examples. They show us how differently people write in terms of style and length. Journal entries are not meant to be long and overly detailed.[9] The following journal entry serves as a model:

1. October 17, 6–7:15 a.m., in the living room (before the kids get up). I feel mostly peaceful about my life.

2. *Contemplatio*: I have thought a great deal about how much God wants us to change. I am aware of many rebellious thoughts and acts. Even yesterday! And I have been wondering if I am brave enough to follow him and change even small things. I have been praying, "Lord, let me recognize your goodness in my life." Yes, I have felt very blessed as I have noticed these many gifts.

3. *Meditatio* on Psalm 139:1–18: God knows me! All of me, even my inward parts. I can't hide from God, and I can't hide anything from God. And God has been near me since my beginning. God has been with me in my times of joy and sorrow.

41

4. *Oratio*: Lord, I feel loved, and also a little naked. It is somewhat disconcerting that I can't keep any secrets from you. But there is a funny peace in this, because you already know me, and because you know all the areas of my life that need to be changed. Lord God, I am amazed at your love and that you have not rejected me.

5. Summary: Where is God's goodness in all this? I recognize God's goodness everywhere! Even my fears "in the darkest places" (vv. 11–12) are answered by God's goodness.

The amount of time you spend in prayer and journaling will fluctuate somewhat. Here are some flexible guidelines: Sections 1 and 2 may take less than ten minutes unless it has been a long time since you have written in your journal. In this case, you may want to devote your entire time to praying about section 2. Section 3 records what happened in your prayer time of forty minutes to an hour, and it may take ten minutes or so to make this record. Sections 4 and 5 may take an additional five to ten minutes. Spend only sixty to ninety minutes on the entire process.

Tom Ashbrook, director of spiritual formation, Church Resource Ministries, reports these three common deficiencies in many journals:

Particularly in the early units, my listening responses have a lot to do with helping folks to faithfully use the prayer time and the journaling method. I have found that if a person follows the method faithfully, then the outcomes are much better. While some try to follow the journaling method faithfully, I find that most do not until I encourage and point out that . . . they failed to mention the grace in #2, or did not really use feeling words in #4, or did not respond to the grace of the unit in #5.[10]

In light of his observations, it is advisable to review your entries regularly to see how faithful you have been to cover all five sections as you are journaling.

Reviewing Your Journal

One of the main uses of the journal is that, like a snapshot, it captures your experience in such a way that you can examine it again. It is of great benefit if you discuss your journal with your listener(s) at the end of each unit. This is not intended to put you on the spot but is meant to open another channel of love and support for you. Very often, disciples are either too hard or too easy on themselves. Listeners can call you to be more realistic in evaluating your experience. When you meet with your listener(s) to review your journal, several guidelines should be observed:

1. Start with a simple prayer, in which you ask Christ to be with you during your review. Ask Christ to give you appreciation and discernment.
2. Follow the instructions for day 7 of the unit you are completing. These include answering specific questions, discussing passages in your journal, and praying together. If there are no specific instructions for your review, briefly summarize each day one at a time. Pause briefly after each day's review and wait for suggestions. Do not be upset if your listeners make no comment at all.
3. Listeners are not supposed to teach you. They listen and offer suggestions only if they are needed.
4. Remember you are seeking the Lord's approval. But do not quickly set aside your listeners' suggestions as Christ may speak to you through your listeners. Do not defend your views or argue with your listeners.
5. Limit your meeting to a reasonable length of time. It is not meant to be another long chat. Generally, an hour should be plenty of time.

4

INSTRUCTIONS
FOR LISTENERS

*S*ACRED *LISTENING* ENCOURAGES disciples to serve as listeners within a listening team. This chapter explains in detail how to be a listener. How do you serve your friend who is sharing from her journal? When do you speak and when do you remain silent? What are the dos and don'ts? These are the sorts of questions this chapter seeks to address.

Listening to other people make these Exercises is a tremendous privilege. I have served as a listener for many people, and each one has challenged me at a profound level with their experience and insight. Sometimes I am confronted by the realization that I fully share their hardness of heart and fears about the spiritual life. More commonly, I am awed by the grace of God as seen in their continued love and courage. Both experiences draw me to review my commitments within the kingdom of God. I suspect you too will discover that you will be stretched by the Holy Spirit as you listen to how the Lord is leading his disciples.

The responsibility of accompanying others on this spiritual journey would greatly discourage all but the most foolish persons if we did not fully believe that *the Holy Spirit is the Spiritual Director of these Exercises.*[1] The Spirit of the living God wants his disciples to grow in grace far more than we do. God has provided all things necessary for our growth in the Scriptures and through the church.[2] The recognition that we are part of God's provision is an inspiring thought that might tempt us to pride. We will do well if we meditate on 2 Corinthians 4, where the apostle Paul reminds us we have the great treasure of God's ministry in clay pots. One of my professors at seminary frequently commented that all of us are "cracked pots," and so the flow of God's gifts through us is even more miraculous. Any feelings of inadequacy in the listening ministry must be wed to the promise that God can and will use us in our weakness. Indeed, our Lord has made provision in his Spirit to intercede for us and through us.[3] My intention in giving these brief instructions is to help persons listen more effectively and compassionately.

A Ministry of Listening

Before proceeding with this section, if you are working in an established program, follow the instructions of your facilitator.

If you are working in a listening team apart from an established program, one disciple reads his journal summary while the other listens. Each takes a turn reading and then serves as listener for the other. If you have a three-person listening team, the third listener is devoted to listening to God and to praying for the one reading her journal. This third listener does not need to say anything at all. Again, each takes a turn reading his or her summary, then functions in turn in both listening roles.

The ministry of listening encouraged by these Exercises is very specific. We are not asked to teach anything or to be responsible for anyone else. We are asked to walk on a spiritual path with other disciples, to offer them encouragement, to hold them accountable to continue praying, and if asked, to provide a reflection or second opinion that will help them appreciate their experience of the love of God. We are called as companions, and thus to share the perceived risks of deepening our relationships with God. Thomas Hart, author of *The Art of Christian Listening*, describes this ministry well:

> The willingness to enter into a helping relationship is essentially the willingness to be a companion—not a teacher, not a savior, but a companion. One agrees to go along. The word "companion" means one who breaks bread with another. People who break bread together share life. It might be nice to be able to do more for someone else—to be savior, wonder-worker, supplier of every need. The helper cannot promise so much, but one gift she or he can give, and that is to be a companion. I will go with you on your journey, take to heart all that concerns you, be there when you need me. This is companionship.[4]

Your ministry as a listening companion will succeed or fail to the degree that you can resist trying to teach spirituality. It cannot be taught by any method with which I am familiar. It must be caught—not taught. Nor are we responsible to teach each other to know the Lord.[5] It is the ministry of the Holy Spirit to reveal Christ to us.[6] Your responsibilities as a listening companion are to listen to the Lord's disciples, to the Lord, and to your own reactions and thoughts.

Responsibilities of Listeners

First, you must make every effort to really hear your praying friends. Appreciate their struggles and disappointments. Revel in their joys and victories. But try to keep a separate perspective so you can accurately reflect their situation back to them. You can help them most by asking questions that help them discover how God is loving them in this situation, and by encouraging them to stay with the journaling process as closely as possible.

Second, you must listen to the Lord, for as a listening companion you have been called into a special kind of intercession. You are asking God to give this disciple an abundant experience of God's love. Your ears, eyes, and heart are given to the task of recognizing God's goodness and mercy as he deals with another person. If you are part of a three-person listening team, this is especially your responsibility when you are serving as the third listener.

Last, you are asked to listen to your own thoughts, motives, and reactions. Judgmental thoughts are especially tricky because they can quickly skew the whole listening process. Another difficulty occurs when you cannot separate your emotions and thoughts from theirs. If either of these happens, confess it immediately and seek outside help. If things seem to be getting off track, you may be facing a number of temptations involving control issues.

Identifying Control Issues

Confronting

You may be tempted to try to move a disciple ahead of our Lord's schedule. It is imperative that we learn that our Lord has his own time for all things, and so we must learn that our role as listening companions calls for patience. We are reminded, as we pray, that we cannot make anything happen in a disciple's life.[7] We recall she is not our disciple — she belongs to the Lord. Ask the Holy Spirit to allow you to be sensitive to God and his schedule. Check your motives and your timing before you intervene in any way. It is especially important to remember that not all issues need to be confronted and that

47

only a few are immediately dangerous. Most issues will come into focus at several points as a disciple prays with the themes suggested in these Exercises.

This temptation can be extreme when a disciple's prayer has been dry for some time and you suspect he is resisting a difficult lesson. Four comments may help.

First, do not assume the disciple knows he is resisting. Often he does not know why he is discontent, unfocused, and dry in his prayer. He may need you to point out the resistance and suggest the problem underlying it. Simple issues can be pointed out in passing. A serious problem calls us to seek the Lord to either address the disciple directly or to prepare the disciple to receive the news from us.[8]

Second, if the problem is not compounding, it is wise to wait until it can be clearly shown to the disciple. This will prevent an initial argument over its reality and soften your errors in judgment.[9]

Third, be very careful about trying to force changes in a disciple's behavior. The disciple belongs to our Lord, and even the delay in behavioral change may be productive in the long run.[10]

Last, do not pull away from your friendship. A disciple needs your companionship at this point most of all.

Counseling

You might be tempted to let your ministry of listening deteriorate into problem solving or therapy.[11] Our purpose in the Exercises is not to become more efficient, more assertive, or more independent. Our purpose is to draw closer to Jesus and to choose his will more consistently. The temptation to salve all sources of discomfort traps us within one of the ironies of modern life. We can satisfy almost all of our needs—and most of our desires—with little or no thought of God. The irony strikes us when we realize that the complete satisfaction of our needs and desires is anesthetic to spiritual life. Blessed are the spiritually desperate, who mourn their attachments and feel empty until each one of their relationships is filled with God's love; who are persecuted, insulted, and misunderstood, for they experience the kingdom of God every day!

Influencing

You might also be tempted to try to influence the outcome of the issues a disciple is praying about. Ignatius himself made some rather direct comments pertinent to this control issue in what is called the Fifteenth Annotation:

> He who is giving the Exercises ought not to influence him who is receiving them more to poverty or to a promise, than to their opposites, nor more to one state or way of life than to another. For though, outside the Exercises, we can lawfully and with merit influence every one who is probably fit to choose continence, virginity, the religious life and all manner of evangelical perfection, still in the Spiritual Exercises, when seeking the Divine Will, it is more fitting and much better, that the Creator and Lord Himself should communicate Himself to His devout soul, inflaming it with His love and praise, and disposing it for the way in which it will be better able to serve Him in the future. So, he who is giving the Exercises should not turn or incline to one side or the other, but standing in the centre like a balance, leave the Creator to act immediately with the creature, and the creature with its Creator and Lord.[12]

Forcing Discernment

One last control issue deserves our attention. You may be tempted to try to force God to bless you with insight for his disciple. You cannot control when God will bless you in this way. Consider this observation by two well-disciplined listeners:

> Some directors believe that their ability to discern is directly related to the amount of time they spend in prayer and fasting. Surely we could all benefit from more in-depth prayer and

self-discipline. But no one merits the grace of discernment. We cannot achieve it by any amount of personal effort.[13]

When the Lord shares with us something that will help his disciple, we are glad for such a gift. We share these things humbly, especially as we advance on the spiritual path ourselves.

Three Additional Suggestions

In your role as a listener, strive to maintain the desirable qualities listed in chapter 2 (pp. 26–27). Three additional suggestions may help you as you begin as a listening companion.

First, in all helping relationships, the need for confidentiality is acute. These Exercises call the disciple to a depth of soul-searching and discovery that can be quite uncomfortable. The Lord's disciple will need to share her discoveries with someone she can trust. Often these discoveries are quite humiliating or painful. You are called to be loving and trustworthy as she shares her pain. Your confidentiality (or lack of it) will be essential to her in confronting her problems and dark secrets. Ask her permission if you need to speak to someone else about something she has shared. Afterward, report that you shared as permitted.

Second, if you are not listening to these Exercises as part of an established discipleship program, I highly recommend that you seek supervision from a pastor or more mature Christian friend. Share with him or her very generally so as not to violate any confidences. Ask this person to pray for and with you.

Third, if training in spiritual direction is available, make the most of your resources and get all the training you can. If you cannot find training and supervision in your community, I recommend contacting the Shalem Institute for Spiritual Formation in Washington, D.C. Their regional meetings and shorter residential programs have been helpful to many listeners.[14] This ministry of listening is greatly needed in the church today.[15]

Listeners should be aware of several guidelines to follow in their meetings with the Lord's disciples:

1. Limit your meeting to a reasonable length of time. It is not meant to be just a good chat. Generally, an hour should be plenty of time. Contacts outside your meeting should not involve discussion of the Exercises, so that the emotional energy is not spent prematurely, and so that others will not overhear what they cannot understand.

2. Meet where you will not be disturbed by unnecessary interruptions, visual distractions, or excessive noise.

3. If you as a listener are not currently making the Exercises yourself, you need to review the assigned Scriptures, Ignatian structures, and Rules for Discernment prior to meeting with the Lord's disciple. This will allow you as a listener to give the disciple your full attention. This is especially important for listeners who have never made the Exercises themselves.

4. Remember, the Holy Spirit is the primary listener. This means you do not need to teach during this meeting. As a *second* listener, you are there to listen and often do not need to say anything at all. As you are led by the Holy Spirit, you may want to reflect back to the disciple(s) what you hear. Listen carefully, and then summarize it with minimal interpretation. "What I hear you saying is . . ." Above all, focus on the question for section 5 of the journal: "Where is the gift you seek from God found in all of this?"

5. Follow the specific instructions for day 7 of the current unit. These instruct you to discuss certain questions as you reflect and pray about the disciple's experience.

6. If you have a three-person listening team, the third listener is devoted to listening to God and to praying for

51

the one reading his or her journal. This third listener does not need to say anything at all. Again, each takes a turn reading his or her summary, then functions in turn in both listening roles.

7. Pray together for continued growth, understanding, and peace as you finish.

PART TWO

Daily Assignments

Or do you despise the riches of His goodness, forbearance, and longsuffering, not knowing that the goodness of God leads you to repentance?

Romans 2:4 NKJV

THE
FIRST
MOVEMENT

UNIT I

■ **Preliminary Comments**

For the best possible beginning to your *Sacred Listening* Exercises, you need a good understanding of the first three sections of chapter 2 as well as a willingness to experience God's abundant goodness. The journaling instructions given with each day are not meant as a straitjacket. Please find your own style in this journaling process.

The goal of unit 1 is to introduce you to a form of contemplative prayer—the *lectio divina*—and to help you taste and see the goodness of God.[1] Allow sixty to ninety minutes for each day's assignment. Begin each prayer time by repeating the assigned theme several times, which will help you focus your mind to pray. As you "center" or become more focused inside, ask the Lord to bless your meditation by giving you the grace suggested for that day. After a few minutes of silence, follow the instructions for prayer. Enjoy your time, even if it is seemingly unproductive or quiet.

THEME: God's goodness is extravagant.

Day **1** **GRACE**: Lord, let me taste your goodness.

In section 1 of your journal, record day, time, place, and condition. Skip section 2 only on your first day. Follow the assignment before recording anything for sections 3–5.

Meditatio: After repeating the theme several times, ask for the grace. Become a secondhand witness of the events in Luke 15:1–7 by reading it "as though it were happening now . . . offer yourself as present to what is said and done by our Lord Jesus Christ with the whole affective power of your mind. . . . Hear and see these things being narrated as though you were hearing with your own ears, and seeing with your own eyes."[2]

After witnessing the passage (and especially the parable), sit in silence for several minutes. After witnessing this three times, ask the Lord again for the grace.

Oratio: Discuss this with the Lord and thank him for loving you.

Review the instructions on keeping your journal (pp. 35–41), and enjoy making your last three entries.

GRACE: Lord, let me experience your generosity. Day **2**

In section 1 of your journal, record day, time, place, and condition.

Contemplatio: In section 2 of your journal, record your experience of the grace from day 1. Follow the assignment before recording anything for sections 3–5.

Meditatio: After repeating the theme several times, ask for the grace. As in day 1, apply your imagination to Matthew 20:1–16 and become a secondhand witness. After witnessing the passage, sit in silence for several minutes. After witnessing this three times, ask the Lord again for the grace.

Oratio: Discuss this with the Lord and thank him for loving you.

Review the instructions on keeping your journal and make your last three entries.

GRACE: Lord, assure me of your care and nearness. Day **3**

In section 1 of your journal, record day, time, place, and condition.

Contemplatio: In section 2 of your journal, record your experience of the grace from day 2. Follow the assignment before recording anything for sections 3–5.

Meditatio: After repeating the theme several times, ask for the grace. Read Romans 8:26–34 three times. Pause for several minutes of silence between each reading.

Oratio: Discuss this with the Lord and thank him for loving you.

Remember to make a brief record of this discussion in section 3 of your journal and then complete the last two entries.

___

Day **4**   **GRACE**: Lord, open my heart to trust your love.

In section 1 of your journal, record day, time, place, and condition.

Contemplatio: In section 2 of your journal, record your experience of the grace from day 3. Follow the assignment before recording anything for sections 3–5.

Meditatio: After repeating the theme several times, ask for the grace. As in day 1, apply your imagination to Luke 11:1–13, and become a secondhand witness. After witnessing the passage, sit in silence for several minutes. After witnessing this three times, ask the Lord again for the grace. Then sit in silence to complete your hour. As you finish, thank Jesus for loving you.

Oratio: Discuss this with the Lord and thank him for loving you.

As you make your last three journal entries, remember to use feeling words in section 4.

___

Day **5**   **GRACE**: Lord, let me believe that you are eager to forgive me.

In section 1 of your journal, record day, time, place, and condition.

Contemplatio: In section 2 of your journal, record your experience of the grace from day 4. Follow the assignment before recording anything for sections 3–5.

Meditatio: After repeating the theme several times, ask for the grace. Read Isaiah 55:1–13 three times, pausing between each reading to wait in silence for several minutes. Consider your own life in terms of God's invitation.

Oratio: Discuss this with the Lord and thank him for loving you.

Complete sections 3–5 of your journal.

GRACE: Lord, let me desire to follow you always.

In section 1 of your journal, record day, time, place, and condition.

Contemplatio: In section 2 of your journal, record your experience of the grace from day 5. Follow the assignment before recording anything for sections 3–5.

Meditatio: After repeating the theme several times, ask for the grace. Read the first and second Rules for Discernment (p. 177) three times, pausing for several minutes between each reading.[3] Ask the Lord to show you which rule describes your life at the present time. Paraphrase the statements that describe your life.

Oratio: Discuss this with the Lord and thank him for the desire he gives you to follow him more closely.

Remember to include your paraphrases in section 3 as you complete your journal entries.

GRACE: Lord, open our hearts to trust your love.

In section 1 of your journal, record day, time, place, and condition.

Contemplatio: In section 2 of your journal, record your experience of the grace from day 6.

Meditatio: Review all six days by reading your journal before you meet with your listener.* Pray and meditate on what you read here. Prepare a brief written summary for your listener. Before you meet with your listener, reread the guidelines for reviewing your journal (p. 43).

Oratio: Meet and share your summary with your listener. Briefly consider which of these graces you are experiencing today. Which do you most want to experience? Pray together and thank God for blessing you.

After meeting with your listener, record any new insights in section 3 and your emotions in section 4 of your journal.

---

*To avoid the tedious repetition of the possible plurals to include listening triads, I omit referring to "listeners" in the instructions for day 7.

UNIT 2

■ **Preliminary Comments**

It is not unusual to feel a nagging distrust of God's meddling in your life. Most of us wonder, "Is God really good?" Deep down we often question what God really wants from us. If this fear goes unchallenged, we may be tempted to leave the spiritual life and seek comfort from other pleasures. The apostle Paul warns us in Romans 2:4 that we should not think lightly of the riches of God's kindness, forbearance, and patience. God's kindness has a specific purpose—it helps us change. This week it is hoped you will discover that God has been with you in times of joy and happiness. We seek to store up encouragement for the journey ahead.[4]

Units 2, 3, and 4 will walk you through an in-depth review of your spiritual history. If you have previously worked through your spiritual history in a careful manner, it would be beneficial to either review your history, add to it, or rework it.

In days 2 through 6 in these next few units, you will find detailed instructions for making charts to begin working through your spiritual history. The charts will be used throughout the Exercises, and afterward, they will be a helpful tool in understanding patterns in your spiritual growth.[5]

Some disciples dislike or feel uncomfortable using the charts assigned in units 2, 3, and 4. If this method of reviewing your life does not work for you, spend some time considering the categories listed. Journal your thoughts in section 3 and discuss them with the Lord in section 4.

Disciples often spend more than an hour on day 2 in each of these units. *It might be wise to plan longer than an hour on these days.*

THEME: God's goodness is extravagant.

GRACE: Lord, let me recognize your goodness in my life.[6]

In section 1 of your journal, record day, time, place, and ^{Day} **1** condition.

Contemplatio: In section 2 of your journal, briefly record your experience of God's love since you met with your listener. Follow these instructions before recording anything for sections 3–5.

Meditatio: After repeating the assigned theme several times, ask for the grace. Read Psalm 23 three times. Pause for several minutes of silence between each reading. With your imagination, picture Jesus caring for you as the psalm describes.

Oratio: Discuss this with the Lord and thank him for his goodness to you.

As you make your last three journal entries, remember to focus on your feelings and emotions in section 4.

In section 1 of your journal, record day, time, place, and ^{Day} **2** condition.

Contemplatio: In section 2 of your journal, record your experience of the theme and grace since your last journal entry.

Meditatio: Today you are asked to begin working through your spiritual history as you reflect upon the course your life has taken. After repeating the assigned theme several times, ask for the grace for this week. Read Romans 2:4 three times: "Or do you despise the riches of His goodness, forbearance, and longsuffering, not knowing that the goodness of God leads you to repentance?" (NKJV). Pause for several minutes of silence between each reading.

In your journal, draw a chart lengthwise with six columns and label it *Unit 2*. Refer to the sample chart on page 183 to help you with the layout. From left to right, label the columns as follows:

Life Stages

Day 2–Experiences of Joy and Goodness

Day 3–Close Relationships

Day 4–My View of God

Day 5–My View of Self

Day 6–My View of Life's Purpose

You will add the rows down the page as you work on your history. Feel free to use more than one page if necessary.

With this unit's theme of God's goodness in mind, ask the Holy Spirit to guide your memory as you review your life, beginning with your childhood. Under the *Life Stages* column, list your age, residence, and occupation (if applicable).[7] Depending on your unique history, you may want to break your life stages down by residence (if you moved); grades in school (elementary, junior high, high school, college); work history; or any combination of factors or events that help you recall a specific time in your life. Space these proportionately, according to the length of time in each stage.

Under the *Day 2* column, summarize your *experiences of joy and goodness* in each life stage. (The other columns are filled out as you continue through the Exercise this week.) The chart serves as section 3 of your journal.

Oratio: Discuss this with the Lord and thank him for his goodness to you.

Record a summary of your discussion in section 4 and summarize your experience of the grace in section 5 in your journal.

Day **3** In section 1 of your journal, record day, time, place, and condition.

Contemplatio: In section 2 of your journal, record your experience of the theme and grace since your last journal entry.

Meditatio: After repeating the assigned theme several times, ask for the grace for this week. Read Psalm 139:1–18 three times. Pause for several minutes of silence between each reading. Make any brief notes about this in section 3 of your journal.

Turn to your unit 2 chart as you consider how well God knows your history. Ask the Holy Spirit to remind you of additional memories of joy and goodness, and record these on your unit 2 chart. After completing any additions to *Day 2*, move on to the *Day 3* column and briefly describe your *close relationships* during these good times in your life stages.

Oratio: Discuss this with the Lord and thank him for his goodness to you.

Record a summary of your discussion in section 4 and summarize your experience of the grace in section 5 in your journal.

In section 1 of your journal, record day, time, place, and condition. ^{Day}**4**

Contemplatio: In section 2 of your journal, record your experience of the theme and grace since your last journal entry.

Meditatio: After repeating the assigned theme several times, ask for the grace for this week. Read Matthew 11:19, and with your imagination, consider how Jesus loved to eat, drink, and enjoy himself at a party. Make any brief notes about this in section 3 of your journal.

Turning to your unit 2 chart, under the *Day 4* column, briefly describe your *view of God* during these joyous times in your life stages.

Oratio: Discuss this with the Lord and thank him for his goodness to you.

Record a summary of your discussion in section 4 and summarize your experience of the grace in section 5 in your journal.

Day 5 In section 1 of your journal, record day, time, place, and condition.

Contemplatio: In section 2 of your journal, record your experience of the theme and grace since your last journal entry.

Meditatio: After repeating the assigned theme several times, ask for the grace for this week. Repeat the assigned theme several times. Read Psalm 8 three times. Pause for several minutes of silence between each reading. Make any brief notes about this in section 3 of your journal.

Turning to your unit 2 chart, under the *Day 5* column, briefly describe your *view of yourself* during these joyous times in your life stages. Thank God for his amazing grace.

Oratio: Discuss this with the Lord and thank him for his goodness to you.

Record a summary of your discussion in section 4 and summarize your experience of the grace in section 5 in your journal.

Day 6 In section 1 of your journal, record day, time, place, and condition.

Contemplatio: In section 2 of your journal, record your experience of the theme and grace since your last journal entry.

Meditatio: After repeating the assigned theme several times, ask for the grace for this week. Repeat the assigned theme several times. Read Matthew 13:44–46 three times. Pause for several minutes of silence between each reading. Make any brief notes about this in section 3 of your journal. Ask the Lord to remind you of your own view of the purpose of life.

Turning to your unit 2 chart, under the *Day 6* column, briefly describe your *view of life's purpose* during these joyous times in your life stages.

Oratio: Discuss this with the Lord and thank him for his goodness to you.

Record a summary of your discussion in section 4 and summarize your experience of the grace in section 5 in your journal.

GRACE: Lord, open our hearts to trust your love.

In section 1 of your journal, record day, time, place, and condition.

Contemplatio: In section 2 of your journal, record your experience of the theme and grace since your last journal entry.

Meditatio: Review all six days by reading your journal before you meet with your listener. Prayerfully consider all of this in light of Romans 2:4. How has your appreciation of God's goodness changed? Prepare a brief written summary for your listener.

Oratio: Meet and share your summary with your listener. With your listener, discuss what you want to do in response to God's goodness. Pray together and thank God for blessing you.

After meeting with your listener, record any new insights in section 3 and your emotions in section 4 of your journal.

Unit 3

■ Preliminary Comments

Sometimes trouble and hardship overtake us through no fault of our own. At other times, our own rebelliousness brings us many difficulties. This unit focuses upon the difficulties we have not caused, while the next unit looks at our times of rebellion. Many of us have a difficult time believing that Jesus would rescue us if we were one of the "lost sheep" in Luke 15:1–7. It is hoped that in the next week you will discover that God has been very close to you in times of trouble and hardship.

Once again, you will be reviewing your life during this unit, so you may want to plan some extra time for day 2.

THEME: God has been with me
during times of trouble.

GRACE: Lord, open my heart to trust your love.

Day **1** In section 1 of your journal, record day, time, place, and condition.

Contemplatio: In section 2 of your journal, briefly record your experience of God's love since you met with your listener.

Meditatio: After repeating the assigned theme several times, ask for the grace. Read Psalm 46 three times. Pause for several minutes of silence between each reading. In section 3 of your journal, consider how Jesus keeps you safe in the midst of trouble. *Consider God's steadfastness in the midst of your suffering.*

Oratio: Discuss this with the Lord and thank him for his loving presence.

Ps. 25

66

Record a summary of your discussion in section 4 and summarize your experience of the grace in section 5 in your journal.

In section 1 of your journal, record day, time, place, and **Day 2** condition.

Contemplatio: In section 2 of your journal, record your experience of the theme and grace since your last journal entry.

Meditatio: Today you are asked to continue to reflect upon the course your life has taken. After repeating the assigned theme several times, ask for the grace for this week. Read Philippians 2:25–30 three times. Pause for several minutes of silence between each reading. Make any brief notes about this in section 3 of your journal.

In your journal, draw another chart lengthwise with six columns and label it *Unit 3*. This chart will be similar to the one you drew for unit 2, except for the *Day 2* column heading. From left to right, label the columns as follows:

Life Stages

Day 2–Experiences of Hardship and Trouble

Day 3–Close Relationships

Day 4–My View of God

Day 5–My View of Self

Day 6–My View of Life's Purpose

With this unit's theme in mind, ask the Holy Spirit to guide your memory as you review your life, beginning with your childhood. Use the same list of life stages under the first column. Of course, you can use more than one page if needed.

Under the *Day 2* column, summarize your *experiences of hardship and trouble* in each life stage.

Oratio: Discuss this with the Lord and thank him for his loving presence.

Record a summary of your discussion in section 4 and summarize your experience of the grace in section 5 in your journal.

Day **3** In section 1 of your journal, record day, time, place, and condition.

Contemplatio: In section 2 of your journal, record your experience of the theme and grace since your last journal entry.

Meditatio: After repeating the assigned theme several times, ask for the grace for this week. Read Isaiah 43:1–7 three times. Pause for several minutes of silence between each reading. Make any brief notes about this in section 3 of your journal.

Ask the Holy Spirit to remind you of additional memories of hardship and trouble, and record these on your unit 3 chart. After completing any additions to *Day 2*, move on to the *Day 3* column and briefly describe your *close relationships* during these hard times in your life stages.

Oratio: Discuss this with the Lord and thank him for his loving presence.

Record a summary of your discussion in section 4 and summarize your experience of the grace in section 5 in your journal.

Day **4** In section 1 of your journal, record day, time, place, and condition.

Contemplatio: In section 2 of your journal, record your experience of the theme and grace since your last journal entry.

Meditatio: After repeating the assigned theme several times, ask for the grace for this week. Read Matthew 8:23–27 three times.[8] Pause for several minutes of silence between each reading. With your imagination, consider how Jesus had compassion on his disciples. Make any brief notes about this in section 3 of your journal.

Turning to your unit 3 chart, under the *Day 4* column, briefly describe your *view of God* during your hard times.

Oratio: Discuss this with the Lord and thank him for his loving presence.

Record a summary of your discussion in section 4 and summarize your experience of the grace in section 5 in your journal.

In section 1 of your journal, record day, time, place, and condition. Day **5**

Contemplatio: In section 2 of your journal, record your experience of the theme and grace since your last journal entry.

Meditatio: After repeating the theme several times, ask for the grace. Read Mark 10:28–31 three times. Pause for several minutes of silence between each reading. Consider how God knows your every trouble. Make any brief notes about this in section 3 of your journal.

Turning to your unit 3 chart, under the *Day 5* column, briefly describe your *view of yourself* during these hard times.

Oratio: Discuss this with the Lord and thank him for his loving presence.

Record a summary of your discussion in section 4 and summarize your experience of the grace in section 5 in your journal.

In section 1 of your journal, record day, time, place, and condition. Day **6**

Contemplatio: In section 2 of your journal, record your experience of the theme and grace since your last journal entry.

Meditatio: After repeating the theme several times, ask for the grace. Read Matthew 6:25–34 three times. Pause for several minutes of silence between each reading. Consider your priorities in times of trouble. Make any brief notes about this in section 3 of your journal. Ask the Lord to remind you of your own view of the purpose of life.

Turning to your unit 3 chart, under the *Day* 6 column, briefly describe your *view of life's purpose* during these troubled times.

Oratio: Discuss this with the Lord and thank him for his loving presence.

Record a summary of your discussion in section 4 and summarize your experience of the grace in section 5 in your journal.

Day **7** GRACE: Lord, open our hearts to trust your love.

In section 1 of your journal, record day, time, place, and condition.

Contemplatio: In section 2 of your journal, record your experience of the theme and grace since your last journal entry.

Meditatio: Review all six days by reading your journal before you meet with your listener. Prayerfully consider all of this in light of Luke 15:1–7. How has your appreciation of God's goodness changed? Prepare a brief written summary for your listener.

Oratio: Meet and share your summary with your listener. With your listener, discuss what you want to do in response to God's goodness. Pray together and thank God for blessing you.

After meeting with your listener, record any new insights in section 3 and your emotions in section 4 of your journal.

UNIT 4

■ Preliminary Comments

In Psalm 62, David claimed that his soul waited in silence during times of oppression. Our experience is often very different than this—our souls are anything but silent! Instead, we cry out in pain and in fear, and we wonder if our sins have brought these calamities upon us. Many of us have a truly difficult time accepting forgiveness from God. In this unit you seek to look at those times in your life when you have been rebellious, and to discover that God's desire to forgive you is greater than all your sin.

You may want to plan some extra time for day 2, as well as day 4 when you will be reviewing your life.

THEME: God has redeemed
even my times of rebellion.

GRACE: Lord, teach me that you are eager to forgive me.[9]

In section 1 of your journal, record day, time, place, and condition. Day **1**

Contemplatio: In section 2 of your journal, briefly record your experience of God's love since you met with your listener. Follow these instructions before recording anything for sections 3–5.

Meditatio: After repeating the theme several times, ask the Lord for the grace. With your imagination, consider Matthew 9:1–8. After witnessing the passage, sit in silence for several minutes. After witnessing this three times, ask the Lord again for the grace. Make any brief notes about this in section 3 of your journal.

Oratio: Discuss this with the Lord and thank him that he also wants to forgive you.

Record a summary of your discussion in section 4 and summarize your experience of the grace in section 5 in your journal.

Day 2 In section 1 of your journal, record day, time, place, and condition.

Contemplatio: In section 2 of your journal, record your experience of the theme and grace since your last journal entry.

Meditatio: After repeating the theme several times, ask for the grace. Read and witness Matthew 9:10–13 three times. Pause for several minutes of silence between each reading. How will you respond to his call? Make any brief notes about this in section 3 of your journal.

In your journal, draw a chart lengthwise with six columns and label it *Unit 4.* Note the changes in the columns for this chart, especially for day 4. Label them as follows:

Life Stages

Day 2–Experiences of Rebellion

Day 3–Close Relationships

Day 4a–My View of God

Day 4b–My View of Self

Day 5–My View of Life's Purpose

With this unit's theme in mind, ask the Lord to guide your memory as you review your life. Make a new list of life stages under the first column. Of course, you can use more than one page if needed.

Under the *Day 2* column, briefly summarize your experiences of *rebellion* in your journal.

Oratio: Discuss this with the Lord and thank him for his love.

Record a summary of your discussion in section 4 and summarize your experience of the grace in section 5 in your journal.

In section 1 of your journal, record day, time, place, and **Day 3** condition.

Contemplatio: In section 2 of your journal, record your experience of the theme and grace since your last journal entry.

Meditatio: After repeating the assigned theme several times, ask for the grace for this week. Read and witness John 8:1–11 three times. Pause for several minutes of silence between each reading. With your imagination, consider the love and tenderness of Jesus as he deals with this woman. Make any brief notes about this in section 3 of your journal.

Ask the Holy Spirit to remind you of any additional memories of rebellion, and record these on your unit 4 chart. After completing any additions to *Day 2*, move on to the *Day 3* column and briefly describe your *close relationships* during these rebellious times in your life stages.

Oratio: Discuss this with the Lord and thank him for his tenderness toward you.

Record a summary of your discussion in section 4 and summarize your experience of the grace in section 5 in your journal.

In section 1 of your journal, record day, time, place, and **Day 4** condition.

Contemplatio: In section 2 of your journal, record your experience of the theme and grace since your last journal entry.

Meditatio: After repeating the assigned theme several times, ask for the grace for this week. Read and witness Matthew 8:1–4 three times. Pause for several minutes of silence between each reading. Recalling how leprosy was considered by many to be a punishment for sin, see how eager Jesus is to encourage this outcast. Make any brief notes about this in section 3 of your journal.

Turning to your unit 4 chart, under the *Day 4a* column, briefly describe your *view of God* during these times of rebellion. In addition, under the *Day 4b* column, describe your *view of yourself* during these temptations.

Oratio: Discuss this with the Lord and thank him for his loving touch in your life. Record a summary of your discussion in section 4 and summarize your experience of the grace in section 5 in your journal.

Day **5** In section 1 of your journal, record day, time, place, and condition.

Contemplatio: In section 2 of your journal, record your experience of the theme and grace since your last journal entry.

Meditatio: After repeating the theme several times, ask for the grace. Read Matthew 11:25–30 three times. Pause for several minutes of silence between each reading. Consider your priorities in times of temptation and rebellion. Ask the Lord to teach you that he is eager to forgive you. Make any brief notes about this in section 3 of your journal.

Turning to your unit 4 chart, under the *Day 5* column, briefly describe your *view of life's purpose* during these trials.

Oratio: Discuss this with the Lord and thank him for his amazing love.

Record a summary of your discussion in section 4 and summarize your experience of the grace in section 5 in your journal.

Day **6** In section 1 of your journal, record day, time, place, and condition.

Contemplatio: In section 2 of your journal, record your experience of the theme and grace since your last journal entry.

Meditatio: Repeat the assigned theme several times and ask for the grace. Read Psalm 32:1–7 three times. Pause for several minutes of silence between each reading. In section 3 of your journal, describe who the Lord is to you at this stage in your journey.

Oratio: Discuss this with the Lord and thank him for his continued goodness.

Record a summary of your discussion in section 4 and summarize your experience of the grace in section 5 in your journal.

GRACE: Lord, open our hearts to trust your love.   Day **7**

In section 1 of your journal, record day, time, place, and condition.

Contemplatio: In section 2 of your journal, record your experience of the theme and grace since your last journal entry.

Meditatio: Review all six days by reading your journal before you meet with your listener. Prayerfully consider: how has your appreciation of God's mercy changed? Prepare a brief written summary for your listener.

Oratio: Meet and share your summary with your listener. With your listener, discuss what you want to do in response to God's goodness. Pray together and thank God for blessing you.

After meeting with your listener, record any new insights in section 3 and your emotions in section 4 of your journal.

UNIT 5

■ **Preliminary Comments**

This week you begin to wrestle with the Principle and Foundation. It is best not to read this Ignatian text until after you complete day 4. The Principle and Foundation summarizes where we are going. Do not worry if you are far from accepting this ideal at the present time. Use the same theme and seek the same grace all week. After all the charting activities in units 2, 3, and 4, you may want to review chapter 3 on journaling. Enjoy your time, even if it is seemingly unproductive or silent.

THEME: God is calling me to live with him.

GRACE: Lord, let me hear and accept your call.

Day **1** In section 1 of your journal, record day, time, place, and condition.

Contemplatio: In section 2 of your journal, briefly record your experience of God's love since you met with your listener.

Meditatio: After repeating the theme several times, ask for the grace. Read Philippians 1:21–30 three times. Pause for several minutes of silence between each reading. If your mind begins to wander, read the text again. Briefly record your meditation in section 3 of your journal.

Oratio: Discuss this with the Lord and thank him for knowing your name.

Record a summary of your discussion in section 4 and summarize your experience of the grace in section 5 in your journal.

In section 1 of your journal, record day, time, place, and ^{Day} **2** condition.

Contemplatio: In section 2 of your journal, record your experience of the theme and grace since your last journal entry.

Meditatio: After repeating the theme several times, ask for the grace. Read Philippians 2:3–8 three times. Pause for several minutes of silence between each reading. If your mind begins to wander, read the text again. Briefly record your meditation in section 3 of your journal.

Oratio: Discuss this with the Lord and thank him for his loving sacrifice.

Record a summary of your discussion in section 4 and summarize your experience of the grace in section 5 in your journal.

In section 1 of your journal, record day, time, place, and ^{Day} **3** condition.

Contemplatio: In section 2 of your journal, record your experience of the theme and grace since your last journal entry.

Meditatio: After repeating the theme several times, ask for the grace. Read Philippians 3:7–15 three times. Pause for several minutes of silence between each reading. If your mind begins to wander, read the text again. Briefly record your meditation in section 3 of your journal.

Oratio: Discuss this with the Lord and thank him for his call in your life.

Record a summary of your discussion in section 4 and summarize your experience of the grace in section 5 in your journal.

In section 1 of your journal, record day, time, place, and ^{Day} **4** condition.

Contemplatio: In section 2 of your journal, record your experience of the theme and grace since your last journal entry.

Meditatio: After repeating the theme several times, ask for the grace. Read Philippians 4:6–13 three times. Pause for several minutes of silence between each reading. If your mind begins to wander, read the text again. Briefly record your meditation in section 3 of your journal.

Oratio: Discuss this with the Lord and thank him for his call in your life.

Record a summary of your discussion in section 4 and summarize your experience of the grace in section 5 in your journal.

Day 5 In section 1 of your journal, record day, time, place, and condition.

Contemplatio: In section 2 of your journal, record your experience of the theme and grace since your last journal entry.

Meditatio: After repeating the theme several times, ask for the grace. Pausing for several minutes of silence between each reading, read the Principle and Foundation (p. 179) at least three times. If your mind begins to wander, read the text again. Briefly record your meditation in section 3 of your journal.

Oratio: Discuss this with the Lord and thank him for his purposeful creation.

Record a summary of your discussion in section 4 and summarize your experience of the grace in section 5 in your journal.

Day 6 In section 1 of your journal, record day, time, place, and condition.

Contemplatio: In section 2 of your journal, record your experience of the theme and grace since your last journal entry.

Meditatio: After repeating the theme several times, ask for the grace. Pausing for several minutes of silence between each reading, read the Principle and Foundation (p. 179) three times. Consider the expression "to find indifference" (see glossary, p. 204). This is not a lack of emotions. Rather, as we become aware of a creative mix in our emotions, we can be objective and impartial as we choose what is best for attaining God's purposes. It may help to rewrite the Principle and Foundation in your own words in section 3 of your journal.

Oratio: Discuss this with the Lord and thank him for his purposeful creation.

Record a summary of your discussion in section 4 and summarize your experience of the grace in section 5 in your journal.

GRACE: Lord, open our hearts to trust your love.   Day **7**

In section 1 of your journal, record day, time, place, and condition.

Contemplatio: In section 2 of your journal, record your experience of the theme and grace since your last journal entry.

Meditatio: Review all six days by reading your journal before you meet with your listener. Prepare a brief written summary for your listener.

Oratio: Meet and share your summary with your listener. With your listener, discuss what you want to do in response to God's call. Pray together and thank God for blessing you.

After meeting with your listener, record any new insights in section 3 and your emotions in section 4 of your journal.

UNIT 6

■ **Preliminary Comments**

Sin is a terrible thing. It becomes even more terrible when set in the context of God's love. The grace we seek this week seems a little odd. Few of us would think of praying for confusion. But we seek a particular kind of confusion, in which we do not understand why we sin against one who is so good to us.[10] God's limitless mercy, goodness, and love cause us to wonder why anyone would choose to rebel against God. As before, begin each prayer time by repeating the assigned theme several times. This will help you focus your mind to pray. As you center and become more focused inside, ask the Lord to bless your meditation by giving you the grace. Enjoy your time, even if it is seemingly unproductive or silent.

> **THEME:** Sin is tragic—its consequences continue beyond what I can see or know.

GRACE: Lord, let me be amazed and confused as I ponder creation's rebellion against your love.

Day **1** In section 1 of your journal, record day, time, place, and condition.

Contemplatio: In section 2 of your journal, briefly record your experience of God's love since you met with your listener.

Meditatio: After repeating the theme several times, ask for the grace. Pausing for several minutes of silence between each reading, read Luke 15:11–32 three times. Using your imagination, place yourself in this story as the prodigal's parent.[11] What do you know, feel, and want to do in each episode

(vv. 11–12, 13, 14–19, 20–24, 25–32)? Briefly record your meditation in section 3 of your journal.

Oratio: Discuss this with the Lord and thank him for his unfailing love.

Record a summary of your discussion in section 4 and summarize your experience of the grace in section 5 in your journal.

In section 1 of your journal, record day, time, place, and condition. Day **2**

Contemplatio: In section 2 of your journal, record your experience of the theme and grace since your last journal entry.

Meditatio: After repeating the theme several times, ask for the grace. Read Jude 6 three times. Pause for several minutes of silence between each reading, and then consider the first sin: Some angels did not continually reverence and obey their Creator and Lord. Instead, they became proud and fell from heaven to hell. For one sin they perished.[12] Briefly record your meditation in section 3 of your journal.

Oratio: Discuss this with the Lord and thank him for his unfailing love.

Record a summary of your discussion in section 4 and summarize your experience of the grace in section 5 in your journal.

In section 1 of your journal, record day, time, place, and condition. Day **3**

Contemplatio: In section 2 of your journal, record your experience of the theme and grace since your last journal entry.

Meditatio: After repeating the theme several times, ask for the grace. Read Genesis 3:1–13 three times. Pause for several minutes of silence between each reading, and then consider the second sin: Adam and Eve were created in love and surrounded with the best possible things. They were given only one prohibition: Do not eat of the Tree of Knowledge. They ate and sinned. Afterward, clothed in tunics of skin and cast from Paradise, they lived all their lives in a ruined state. They lived with many labors and much suffering and repentance.[13] Briefly record your meditation in section 3 of your journal.

Oratio: Discuss this with the Lord and thank him for his unfailing love.

Record a summary of your discussion in section 4 and summarize your experience of the grace in section 5 in your journal.

Day **4** In section 1 of your journal, record day, time, place, and condition.

Contemplatio: In section 2 of your journal, record your experience of the theme and grace since your last journal entry.

Meditatio: After repeating the theme several times, ask for the grace. Pausing between readings for a few minutes of silence, read the third and fourth Rules for Discernment[14] (p. 178) three times. In section 3 of your journal, using your imagination, list possible experiences of *consolation* and *desolation* as defined in these rules.

Oratio: Discuss your experiences of consolation and desolation with the Lord and thank him for his unfailing love.

Record a summary of your discussion in section 4 and summarize your experience of the grace in section 5 in your journal.

Day **5** In section 1 of your journal, record day, time, place, and condition.

Contemplatio: In section 2 of your journal, record your experience of the theme and grace since your last journal entry.

Meditatio: After repeating the theme several times, ask for the grace. Read Genesis 3:17–19 three times. Pause for several minutes of silence between each reading. Meditate on the effects of disobedience upon creation. Briefly record your meditation in section 3 of your journal.

Oratio: Discuss your thoughts, emotions, and desires with the Lord.

Record a summary of your discussion in section 4 and summarize your experience of the grace in section 5 in your journal.

In section 1 of your journal, record day, time, place, and condition. _{Day} **6**

Contemplatio: In section 2 of your journal, record your experience of the theme and grace since your last journal entry.

Meditatio: After repeating the theme several times, ask for the grace. Read Luke 15:11–32. Using your imagination, place yourself in this story as the prodigal's older brother. As you witness the events or hear them reported by travelers and gossips, what do you know, feel, and want to do in each episode (vv. 11–12, 13, 14–19, 20–24, 25–32)? After your meditation, consider how the brother's reactions illustrate the tragedy of sin. Briefly record your meditation in section 3 of your journal.

Oratio: Discuss your thoughts, emotions, and desires with the Lord.

Record a summary of your discussion in section 4 and summarize your experience of the grace in section 5 in your journal.

GRACE: Lord, open our hearts to trust your love. Day **7**

In section 1 of your journal, record day, time, place, and condition.

Contemplatio: In section 2 of your journal, record your experience of the theme and grace since your last journal entry.

Meditatio: Review all six days by reading your journal before you meet with your listener. Prayerfully consider: how has your appreciation of God's mercy changed? Prepare a brief written summary for your listener.

Oratio: Meet and share your summary with your listener. With your listener, discuss what you want to do in response to God's love. Pray together and thank God for blessing you.

After meeting with your listener, record any new insights in section 3 and your emotions in section 4 of your journal.

UNIT 7

■ **Preliminary Comments**

Unit 7 deepens our meditation on sin. As before, begin each prayer time by repeating the assigned theme several times. This will help you focus your mind to pray. As you center and become more focused inside, ask the Lord to bless your meditation by giving you the grace. Enjoy your time, even if it is seemingly unproductive or silent.

THEME: We who have sinned much, love much.

GRACE: Lord, give me a growing and intense sorrow for my sins, balanced by a deepening awareness of your merciful love.[15]

In section 1 of your journal, record day, time, place, and **Day 1** condition.

Contemplatio: In section 2 of your journal, briefly record your experience of God's love since you met with your listener.

Meditatio: After repeating the theme several times, ask for the grace. Read Luke 16:19–31 three times. Pause for several minutes of silence between each reading. Using your imagination, place yourself in this story as the rich man. What do you feel, know, and want to do? Briefly record your meditation in section 3 of your journal.

Oratio: Discuss your thoughts, emotions, and desires with the Lord.

Record a summary of your discussion in section 4 and summarize your experience of the grace in section 5 in your journal.

Day 2 In section 1 of your journal, record day, time, place, and condition.

Contemplatio: In section 2 of your journal, record your experience of the theme and grace since your last journal entry.

Meditatio: After repeating the theme several times, ask for the grace. Read 2 Samuel 11:1–12:15 twice. Pause for several minutes of silence between each reading. David is blind to his real sin until he is confronted by Nathan. Ask yourself, "How am I blind like David?" Briefly record your meditation in section 3 of your journal.

Oratio: Discuss your thoughts, emotions, and desires with the Lord.

Record a summary of your discussion in section 4 and summarize your experience of the grace in section 5 in your journal.

Day 3 In section 1 of your journal, record day, time, place, and condition.

Contemplatio: In section 2 of your journal, record your experience of the theme and grace since your last journal entry.

Meditatio: After repeating the theme several times, ask for the grace. Read Luke 15:11–32 three times. Pause for several minutes of silence between each reading. Using your imagination, place yourself in this story as the prodigal child. What do you know, feel, and want to do in each episode (vv. 11–12, 13, 14–19, 20–24, 25–32)? Briefly record your meditation in section 3 of your journal.

Oratio: Discuss this with the Lord and thank him again for a love we cannot understand.

Record a summary of your discussion in section 4 and summarize your experience of the grace in section 5 in your journal.

In section 1 of your journal, record day, time, place, and ^{Day}**4** condition.

Contemplatio: In section 2 of your journal, record your experience of the theme and grace since your last journal entry.

Meditatio: After repeating the theme several times, ask for the grace. Read Psalm 96:1–10 three times. Pause for several minutes of silence between each reading. Then consider who God is, against whom you have sinned, comparing his attributes with their contraries in you—God's wisdom with your ignorance; God's omnipotence with your weakness; God's justice with your iniquity; God's goodness with your malice.[16] Briefly record your meditation in section 3 of your journal.

Oratio: Discuss this with the Lord and thank him again for a love we cannot understand.

Record a summary of your discussion in section 4 and summarize your experience of the grace in section 5 in your journal.

In section 1 of your journal, record day, time, place, and ^{Day}**5** condition.

Contemplatio: In section 2 of your journal, record your experience of the theme and grace since your last journal entry.

Meditatio: After repeating the theme several times, ask for the grace. Read John 15:1–6 three times. Pause for several minutes of silence between each reading. Consider your life apart from Christ. Would you have any hope without his love?

Oratio: Discuss this question with the Lord and thank him again for a love we cannot understand.

Record summaries of your meditation in section 3, your discussion in section 4, and your experience of the grace in section 5 in your journal.

Day 6 In section 1 of your journal, record day, time, place, and condition.

Contemplatio: In section 2 of your journal, record your experience of the theme and grace since your last journal entry.

Meditatio: After repeating the theme several times, ask for the grace. Read Luke 7:36–50 three times.[17] Pause for several minutes of silence between each reading. Using your imagination, place yourself in this story as this woman. How is your life changed by Jesus's love?

Oratio: Discuss this question with the Lord and thank him again for a love we cannot understand.

Record summaries of your meditation in section 3, your discussion in section 4, and your experience of the grace in section 5 in your journal.

Day 7 GRACE: Lord, open our hearts to trust your love.

In section 1 of your journal, record day, time, place, and condition.

Contemplatio: In section 2 of your journal, record your experience of the theme and grace since your last journal entry.

Meditatio: Review all six days by reading your journal before you meet with your listener. Prayerfully consider: how has your appreciation of God's mercy changed? Prepare a brief written summary for your listener.

Oratio: Meet and share your summary with your listener. With your listener, discuss what you want to do in response to God's love. Pray together and thank God for blessing you.

After meeting with your listener, record any new insights in section 3 and your emotions in section 4 of your journal.

UNIT 8

■ **Preliminary Comments**

The apostle Paul makes this observation in 2 Corinthians 7:10–11: "Godly sorrow brings repentance that leads to salvation and leaves no regret, but worldly sorrow brings death" (NIV). Our task this week is to discover some of the reasons we sin, for we are called to "godly sorrow" and repentance. Only a growing sense of God's love and a deepening desire to serve God confirm that we will be ready for unit 9. You may want to plan extra time for day 7 when you will be doing a more extensive review.

THEME: God will show me some
of the hidden sinful tendencies influencing my life.

GRACE: Lord, help me feel and trust that you are eager to forgive me.[18]

In section 1 of your journal, record day, time, place, and **Day 1** condition.

Contemplatio: In section 2 of your journal, briefly record your experience of God's love since you met with your listener.

Meditatio: After repeating the theme several times, ask for the grace. Read Luke 14:16–24 three times. Pause for several minutes of silence between each reading. Ask again for the grace, and then ask, "What hinders me from fully enjoying God's party?"

Oratio: Discuss this question with the Lord and thank him again for a love we cannot understand.

Record summaries of your meditation in section 3, your discussion in section 4, and your experience of the grace in section 5 in your journal.

Day **2** In section 1 of your journal, record day, time, place, and condition.

Contemplatio: In section 2 of your journal, record your experience of the theme and grace since your last journal entry.

Meditatio: After repeating the theme several times, ask for the grace. Read Matthew 15:10–19 three times. Pause for several minutes of silence between each reading. Briefly record your meditation in section 3 of your journal.

Oratio: Discuss your own experience of inner evil with the Lord and thank him because he is eager to forgive you.

Record a summary of your discussion in section 4 and summarize your experience of the grace in section 5 in your journal.

Day **3** In section 1 of your journal, record day, time, place, and condition.

Contemplatio: In section 2 of your journal, record your experience of the theme and grace since your last journal entry.

Meditatio: After repeating the theme several times, ask for the grace. Read Psalm 25:1–7 three times. Pause for several minutes of silence between each reading. Then meditate on the fifth Rule for Discernment (p. 178).[19] Read it again and again. In section 3, journal about a time when you faced desolation and had to make a major decision.

Oratio: Discuss this with the Lord and thank him because he is eager to help you in all good things.

Record a summary of your discussion in section 4 and summarize your experience of the grace in section 5 in your journal.

In section 1 of your journal, record day, time, place, and ^{Day}**4** condition.

Contemplatio: In section 2 of your journal, record your experience of the theme and grace since your last journal entry.

Meditatio: After repeating the theme several times, ask for the grace. Read 1 Peter 5:8–9 several times and consider how it supports this sixth Rule for Discernment (p. 178).[20] In section 3 of your journal, describe a time when you acted as the sixth rule counsels.

Oratio: Discuss this with the Lord and thank him because he is eager to help you in all good things.

Record a summary of your discussion in section 4 and summarize your experience of the grace in section 5 in your journal.

In section 1 of your journal, record day, time, place, and ^{Day}**5** condition.

Contemplatio: In section 2 of your journal, record your experience of the theme and grace since your last journal entry.

Meditatio: Using your imagination, journey to hell. Describe what you see, hear, taste, feel, and smell.[21] With your imagination, consider how long an eternal stay in hell would be. Consider what excuses those in hell may have offered to God. Carefully note your observations and responses in section 3 of your journal.

Oratio: Discuss this with the Lord and thank him for his mercy toward you.

Record a summary of your discussion in section 4 and summarize your experience of the grace in section 5 in your journal.

In section 1 of your journal, record day, time, place, and ^{Day}**6** condition.

Contemplatio: In section 2 of your journal, record your experience of the theme and grace since your last journal entry.

Meditatio: After repeating the theme several times, ask for the grace. Read Psalm 51 three times. Pause for several minutes of silence between each reading.

Oratio: Pray verses 1–12 and let each first person pronoun (I, me) refer to you. Agree with the Lord that you are forgiven. Thank him for his mercy. Stay with the psalm until it is real for you.

Record summaries of your meditation in section 3, your discussion in section 4, and your experience of the grace in section 5 in your journal.

Day **7**   **GRACE:** Lord, open our hearts to trust your love.

In section 1 of your journal, record day, time, place, and condition.

Contemplatio: In section 2 of your journal, record your experience of the theme and grace since your last journal entry.

Meditatio: Review all six days by reading your journal before you meet with your listener. Prayerfully consider: how has your appreciation of God's mercy changed? Prepare a brief written summary for your listener. It may be helpful to make a chart summarizing your most significant experiences, your close relationships, and your view of God, self, and life's purposes in units 6–8 (similar to the Sample Chart for Unit 2 on p. 183).

Oratio: Meet and share your summary with your listener. With your listener, discuss your experience of God's love in this first Ignatian movement. Pray together and thank God for blessing you.

After meeting with your listener, record any new insights in section 3 and your emotions in section 4 of your journal.

SUMMARY OF THE
FIRST MOVEMENT

Unit 8 ends the first Ignatian Movement. Ignatius felt most persons could profit from making the good confession encouraged by these first meditations. Early directories for the *Spiritual Exercises* encouraged disciples to make a general confession of sin at the conclusion of this first movement.[22] Please weigh the value of this. If you have a profound sense of being loved and forgiven—if unit 8, day 6, is very real for you—you may not need to make further confession. If unit 8, day 6, is less real for you, you may gain additional confidence of God's love and forgiveness by confessing your sins "one to another."

If your congregation does not use a particular form for confession, then read James 5:16 and 1 John 1:9. The first text calls us to confess our sins and the second tells us how. In confession, we are not telling the Lord something he does not know. The Greek word for "confess" means to "say the same thing as" or agree with someone about something. We are agreeing with the Lord that we have done these things and that they are indeed wrong. And we are agreeing we have not done things we should have done. Ask a trusted friend to keep your confidence, and then name your sins and agree they are sinful. Ask her or him to remind you that you are deeply loved by God and, as promised in 1 John 1:9, completely forgiven of your sins. Ask your friend to pray for you in the days and weeks to come as you trust more in God's love and change your ways.

THE
SECOND
MOVEMENT

INTRODUCTION TO THE
SECOND MOVEMENT

Having finished unit 8, each person must ask for peace and a sense of call before proceeding into the second Ignatian Movement. Your sense of call may come through meditating on these questions: Do I want the Principle and Foundation to describe my life? Focus on the last paragraph: Is it my deepest desire to live continually in the loving presence and wisdom of Christ, our Savior?[1]

If you have little desire for this at the present time, *please wait* until you have a deep sense of God's love and forgiveness before you attempt to pray with units 9–24. Continue to pray for the gracious gifts you sought in the first four units and wait until the Holy Spirit calls this deep desire forth in your life. There are any number of things you can do while you are waiting.

You may want to repeat units 1–4 and add to your charts. In this case, continue to meet with your listener and discuss the two diagnostic questions given above as you finish unit 4.

You may want to seek help from your pastor or a trained spiritual director and ask him or her to help you understand your lack of confidence in God's love.

You may want to set these Exercises aside and pursue other spiritual reading. The Holy Spirit does not call everyone into the second movement, and there is no shame or failure in choosing to grow in other areas of your life with Christ.

If your deep desire is to live continually in the loving presence and wisdom of Christ, now is a good time to ask for courage for the days ahead. Our focus shifts from our Lord's healing presence to understanding his wisdom. We seek to understand his life and passion as a pattern for our own discipleship. Of course, his loving presence continues always with us as he calls, "Come and follow me."

UNIT 9

■ **Preliminary Comments**

If we have exercised well, then we are ready at this point to begin to appreciate the mystery of Christ coming to live with, and even save, sinners. Because units 6–8 are so intense, many people feel a letdown at the beginning of unit 9.[2] If this was your experience, press on. It will be short-lived, because our goal this week is to simply be overwhelmed with the love of God—God sent Jesus into the humblest and most dangerous circumstances for us.

As you enter the second movement of these Exercises, you may notice your time in prayer is beginning to change. In earlier prayer periods, you have had much to think about as you have entered your prayer time. Much of this early experience can be described as discursive meditation.[3] In weeks to come, it is common for the Holy Spirit to move you into deeper forms of contemplation as you spend longer times of silence during your prayer time. Thank God for these quiet times, and enjoy being present to the Lord.

Please reread Using Your Imagination (pp. 23–24) if your conscience is sensitive about using your imagination in prayer. Your use of imagination here is only to orient your point of view. You are not asked to change anything in the text. It may be helpful to review all of chapters 2 and 3 before you begin.

THEME: The Word was made flesh for me.

GRACE: Lord, give me deep joy in your humanity, that I might love you more and follow you more closely.

In section 1 of your journal, record day, time, place, and ᴰᵃʸ **1** condition.

97

Contemplatio: In section 2 of your journal, briefly record your experience of God's love since you met with your listener.

Meditatio: After repeating the theme several times, ask for the grace. Pausing for several minutes of silence between each reading, read Acts 2:22–24 three times. Christ came according to the predetermined plan of God. Consider how, when, and for whom this plan was made.

Oratio: Wonder with Jesus how this plan affects you and thank him for sharing your humanity.

Record summaries of your meditation in section 3, your discussion in section 4, and your experience of the grace in section 5 in your journal.

Day **2** In section 1 of your journal, record day, time, place, and condition.

Contemplatio: In section 2 of your journal, record your experience of the theme and grace since your last journal entry.

Meditatio: After repeating the theme several times, ask for the grace. Pausing for several minutes of silence between each reading, read Matthew 1:18–25 three times. Briefly record your meditation in section 3 of your journal.

Oratio: Discuss this with the Lord and thank him for sharing your humanity.

Record a summary of your discussion in section 4 and summarize your experience of the grace in section 5 in your journal.

Day **3** In section 1 of your journal, record day, time, place, and condition.

Contemplatio: In section 2 of your journal, record your experience of the theme and grace since your last journal entry.

Meditatio: After repeating the theme several times, ask for the grace. Pausing for several minutes of silence between each reading, read Luke 1:26–38 three times.[4] Briefly record your meditation in section 3 of your journal.

Oratio: Discuss this with the Lord and thank him for sharing your humanity.

Record a summary of your discussion in section 4 and summarize your experience of the grace in section 5 in your journal.

In section 1 of your journal, record day, time, place, and Day **4** condition.

Contemplatio: In section 2 of your journal, record your experience of the theme and grace since your last journal entry.

Meditatio: After repeating the theme several times, ask for the grace. Pausing for several minutes of silence between each reading, read Luke 1:39–55 three times.[5] Meditate especially on verses 46–55. Briefly record your meditation in section 3 of your journal.

Oratio: Discuss this with the Lord and thank him for sharing your humanity.

Record a summary of your discussion in section 4 and summarize your experience of the grace in section 5 in your journal.

In section 1 of your journal, record day, time, place, and Day **5** condition.

Contemplatio: In section 2 of your journal, record your experience of the theme and grace since your last journal entry.

Meditatio: After repeating the theme several times, ask for the grace. Pausing for several minutes of silence between each reading, read Luke 2:1–7 three times.[6] Imagine yourself as some insignificant slave who helped in the birth of Jesus.[7] Briefly record your meditation in section 3 of your journal.

Oratio: Discuss this with the Lord and thank him for sharing your humanity.

Record a summary of your discussion in section 4 and summarize your experience of the grace in section 5 in your journal.

Day **6** In section 1 of your journal, record day, time, place, and condition.

Contemplatio: In section 2 of your journal, record your experience of the theme and grace since your last journal entry.

Meditatio: After repeating the theme several times, ask for the grace. Pausing for several minutes of silence between each reading, read Luke 2:8–20 three times.[8] Imagine yourself as an unimportant shepherd and see how Jesus's family shares your poverty.[9] Briefly record your meditation in section 3 of your journal.

Oratio: Discuss this with the Lord and thank him for sharing your humanity.

Record a summary of your discussion in section 4 and summarize your experience of the grace in section 5 in your journal.

Day **7** If you are making these Exercises just before the Christmas season, you may want to spend another week with the following additional meditations before you review your journal. You can meet after unit 9, day 6, or wait until after the additional meditations in unit 9A (Optional). Remember to meet with your listener with the following plan for day 7 before you begin unit 10.

GRACE: Lord, open our hearts to trust your love.

In section 1 of your journal, record day, time, place, and condition.

Contemplatio: In section 2 of your journal, record your experience of the theme and grace since your last journal entry.

Meditatio: Review all six days by reading your journal before you meet with your listener. Prepare a brief written summary for your listener.

Oratio: Meet and share your summary with your listener. Discuss how the theme and grace for this unit are seen in your meditations. Pray together and thank God for blessing you.

After meeting with your listener, record any new insights in section 3 and your emotions in section 4 of your journal.

Unit 9A (Optional)

■ Preliminary Comments

If you are making these Exercises just before the Christmas season, or if you want to extend the Exercises an extra week, here are additional meditations on the Lord's incarnation.

THEME: The Word was made flesh for me.

GRACE: Lord, give me deep joy in your humanity that I might love you more and follow you more closely.

■ Additional Days

In section 1 of your journal, record day, time, place, and **Day 1** condition.

Contemplatio: In section 2 of your journal, briefly record your experience of God's love since you met with your listener.

Meditatio: After repeating the theme several times, ask for the grace. Pausing for several minutes of silence between each reading, read Luke 2:1–7 three times. Using your imagination, be Mary. How do you respond to the Lord?

Oratio: Discuss this question with the Lord and thank him for sharing your humanity.

Record summaries of your meditation in section 3, your discussion in section 4, and your experience of the grace in section 5 in your journal.

In section 1 of your journal, record day, time, place, and **Day 2** condition.

Contemplatio: In section 2 of your journal, record your experience of the theme and grace since your last journal entry.

Meditatio: After repeating the theme several times, ask for the grace. Pausing for several minutes of silence between each reading, read Luke 2:1–7 three times. Using your imagination, be Joseph. How do you respond to the Lord?

Oratio: Discuss this question with the Lord and thank him for sharing your humanity.

Record summaries of your meditation in section 3, your discussion in section 4, and your experience of the grace in section 5 in your journal.

Day **3** In section 1 of your journal, record day, time, place, and condition.

Contemplatio: In section 2 of your journal, record your experience of the theme and grace since your last journal entry.

Meditatio: After repeating the theme several times, ask for the grace. Pausing for several minutes of silence between each reading, read John 1:1–5 three times. Briefly record your meditation in section 3 of your journal.

Oratio: Discuss this with the Lord and thank him for sharing your humanity.

Record a summary of your discussion in section 4 and summarize your experience of the grace in section 5 in your journal.

Day **4** In section 1 of your journal, record day, time, place, and condition.

Contemplatio: In section 2 of your journal, record your experience of the theme and grace since your last journal entry.

Meditatio: After repeating the theme several times, ask for the grace. Pausing for several minutes of silence between each reading, read Luke 2:1–20 three times. Imagine yourself as one of the angels and describe the events from heaven's perspective.[10] Has there been great celebration or mourning?

Oratio: Discuss this question with the Lord and thank him for sharing your humanity.

Record summaries of your meditation in section 3, your discussion in section 4, and your experience of the grace in section 5 in your journal.

In section 1 of your journal, record day, time, place, and Day **5** condition.

Contemplatio: In section 2 of your journal, record your experience of the theme and grace since your last journal entry.

Meditatio: After repeating the theme several times, ask for the grace. Pausing for several minutes of silence between each reading, read Luke 2:21 three times.[11] Consider the circumcision and naming of Jesus. What does this event mean in your experience today?

Oratio: Discuss this question with the Lord and thank him for sharing your humanity.

Record summaries of your meditation in section 3, your discussion in section 4, and your experience of the grace in section 5 in your journal.

In section 1 of your journal, record day, time, place, and Day **6** condition.

Contemplatio: In section 2 of your journal, record your experience of the theme and grace since your last journal entry.

Meditatio: After repeating the theme several times, ask for the grace. Pausing for several minutes of silence between each reading, read Luke 2:22–38 three times.[12] Using your imagination to be a humble servant, go with Mary and Joseph to present Jesus in the temple. Briefly record your meditation in section 3 of your journal.

Oratio: Discuss this with the Lord and thank him for sharing your humanity.

Record a summary of your discussion in section 4 and summarize your experience of the grace in section 5 in your journal.

Day **7** In section 1 of your journal, record day, time, place, and condition.

Contemplatio: In section 2 of your journal, record your experience of the theme and grace since your last journal entry.

Meditatio: After repeating the theme several times, ask for the grace. Pausing for several minutes of silence between each reading, read Matthew 2:1–12 three times.[13] With your imagination, accompany the wise men as they pay homage to Jesus. Consider the poverty into which he is born.[14] Briefly record your meditation in section 3 of your journal.

Oratio: Discuss this with the Lord and thank him for sharing your humanity.

Record a summary of your discussion in section 4 and summarize your experience of the grace in section 5 in your journal. Remember to meet with your listener as noted earlier in unit 9, day 7.

UNIT 10

■ **Preliminary Comments**

Hebrews 5:8 tells us that Jesus learned obedience from the things that he suffered. We should feel awe at his trials. They were real. He suffered. This week we observe the close relationship God keeps with his Son. Because we have so little information about the early life of Christ, this unit requires a greater use of your imagination. Ask the Holy Spirit to guide you, and then pray as you are able. Do not force anything.

> **THEME:** Jesus learned obedience
> from the things that he suffered.

GRACE: Holy Spirit, teach me how the Lord Jesus suffered many difficulties for me.

In section 1 of your journal, record day, time, place, and ^Day **1** condition.

Contemplatio: In section 2 of your journal, briefly record your experience of God's love since you met with your listener.

Meditatio: After repeating the theme several times, ask for the grace. Pausing for several minutes of silence between each reading, read Matthew 2:13–18 three times.[15] You may find it helpful to discuss some of your own childhood traumas.

Oratio: Discuss this with the Lord and thank him for suffering for you.

Record summaries of your meditation in section 3, your discussion in section 4, and your experience of the grace in section 5 in your journal.

Day 2 In section 1 of your journal, record day, time, place, and condition.

Contemplatio: In section 2 of your journal, record your experience of the theme and grace since your last journal entry.

Meditatio: After repeating the theme several times, ask for the grace. Pausing for several minutes of silence between each reading, read Luke 2:41–50 three times.[16] Once again, become a secondhand witness of the events by reading "as though it were happening now. . . . Offer yourself as present to what is said and done by our Lord Jesus Christ with the whole affective power of your mind. . . . Hear and see these things being narrated as though you were hearing with your own ears, and seeing with your own eyes."[17]

Briefly record your meditation in section 3 of your journal.

Oratio: Discuss this with the Lord and thank him for suffering for you.

Record a summary of your discussion in section 4 and summarize your experience of the grace in section 5 in your journal.

Day 3 In section 1 of your journal, record day, time, place, and condition.

Contemplatio: In section 2 of your journal, record your experience of the theme and grace since your last journal entry.

Meditatio: After repeating the theme several times, ask for the grace. Pausing for several minutes of silence between each reading, read Luke 2:51–52 and Hebrews 2:14–18 three times.[18] With your imagination, think about Jesus's young adult years. Briefly record your meditation in section 3 of your journal.

Oratio: Discuss this with the Lord and thank him for suffering for you.

Record a summary of your discussion in section 4 and summarize your experience of the grace in section 5 in your journal.

In section 1 of your journal, record day, time, place, and ^{Day} **4**
condition.

Contemplatio: In section 2 of your journal, record your experience of the theme and grace since your last journal entry.

Meditatio: After repeating the theme several times, ask for the grace. Pausing for several minutes of silence between each reading, read Matthew 3:13–17 three times.[19] Witness his baptism and consolation. Briefly record your meditation in section 3 of your journal.

Oratio: Discuss the joy of obedience with the Lord and thank him for suffering for you.

Record a summary of your discussion in section 4 and summarize your experience of the grace in section 5 in your journal.

In section 1 of your journal, record day, time, place, and ^{Day} **5**
condition.

Contemplatio: In section 2 of your journal, record your experience of the theme and grace since your last journal entry.

Meditatio: After repeating the theme several times, ask for the grace. Pausing for several minutes of silence between each reading, read Matthew 4:1–11 three times.[20] Witness Jesus as he is tempted in the desert. Briefly record your meditation in section 3 of your journal.

Oratio: Discuss the joy of obedience with the Lord and thank him for suffering for you.

Record a summary of your discussion in section 4 and summarize your experience of the grace in section 5 in your journal.

Day **6** In section 1 of your journal, record day, time, place, and condition.

Contemplatio: In section 2 of your journal, record your experience of the theme and grace since your last journal entry.

Meditatio: After repeating the theme several times, ask for the grace. Pausing for several minutes of silence between each reading, read 1 Corinthians 10:13 and see how it supports these seventh and eighth Rules for Discernment (p. 178).[21] Carefully consider these rules and identify an experience in your life when you felt alone, and still resisted sinful ideas. Briefly record your meditation in section 3 of your journal.

Oratio: Discuss this with the Lord and thank him for providing loving help in your moments of trial.

Record a summary of your discussion in section 4 and summarize your experience of the grace in section 5 in your journal.

Day **7** GRACE: Lord, open our hearts to trust your love.

In section 1 of your journal, record day, time, place, and condition.

Contemplatio: In section 2 of your journal, record your experience of the theme and grace since your last journal entry.

Meditatio: Review all six days by reading your journal before you meet with your listener. Prepare a brief written summary for your listener.

Oratio: Meet and share your summary with your listener. Discuss how the theme and grace for this unit are seen in your meditations. Pray together and thank God for blessing you.

After meeting with your listener, record any new insights in section 3 and your emotions in section 4 of your journal.

Unit 11

■ Preliminary Comments

Ignatius gives us several very profitable parables that were drawn from his culture. The story of the Pilgrim King—or Kingdom Exercise—allows us to step back a short distance and see the gospel with new eyes. Our call in this exercise is not to accept Jesus as Savior but to recognize his love for our broken and battered world. We ask to hear his call and we ask to be called to serve with our servant King. We are asking to be open and generous as we respond to Christ's invitation to live as he lived.[22]

> **THEME:** Jesus is calling me
> to follow and serve with him.

GRACE: Lord, let me hear and accept your call in the unique and concrete circumstances of my life.[23]

In section 1 of your journal, record day, time, place, and ^Day **1** condition.

Contemplatio: In section 2 of your journal, briefly record your experience of God's love since you met with your listener.

Meditatio: After repeating the theme several times, ask for the grace. Pausing for several minutes of silence between each reading, read Mark 1:14–15 three times. Spend at least thirty minutes considering the invitation found in the Kingdom Exercise, Part One (p. 180).

Oratio: Discuss your response with the Lord and thank him for his call in your life.

Record summaries of your meditation in section 3, your discussion in section 4, and your experience of the grace in section 5 in your journal.

Day 2 In section 1 of your journal, record day, time, place, and condition.

Contemplatio: In section 2 of your journal, record your experience of the theme and grace since your last journal entry.

Meditatio: After repeating the theme several times, ask for the grace. Pausing for several minutes of silence between each reading, read Luke 4:14–32 three times. Briefly record your meditation in section 3 of your journal.

Oratio: Discuss your hopes and fears with the Lord and thank him for his call in your life.

Record a summary of your discussion in section 4 and summarize your experience of the grace in section 5 in your journal.

Day 3 In section 1 of your journal, record day, time, place, and condition.

Contemplatio: In section 2 of your journal, record your experience of the theme and grace since your last journal entry.

Meditatio: After repeating the theme several times, ask for the grace. Pausing for several minutes of silence between each reading, read John 1:35–51 three times and apply all five of your senses as you witness the call of Jesus's disciples. Remember that they *were* following a truly good human leader. Briefly record your meditation in section 3 of your journal.

Oratio: Discuss your response with the Lord and thank him for his call in your life.

Record a summary of your discussion in section 4 and summarize your experience of the grace in section 5 in your journal.

In section 1 of your journal, record day, time, place, and condition.

Contemplatio: In section 2 of your journal, record your experience of the theme and grace since your last journal entry.

Meditatio: After repeating the theme several times, ask for the grace. Pausing for several minutes of silence between each reading, read Matthew 8:18–22 three times. Meditate upon these verses in the context of Part One of the Kingdom Exercise (p. 180). Briefly record your meditation in section 3 of your journal.

Oratio: Discuss your response with the Lord and thank him for his call in your life.

Record a summary of your discussion in section 4 and summarize your experience of the grace in section 5 in your journal.

In section 1 of your journal, record day, time, place, and condition.

Contemplatio: In section 2 of your journal, record your experience of the theme and grace since your last journal entry.

Meditatio: After repeating the theme several times, ask for the grace. Pausing for several minutes of silence between each reading, read Matthew 10:16–24 three times. Meditate upon these verses in the context of Part One of the Kingdom Exercise (p. 180). Briefly record your meditation in section 3 of your journal.

Oratio: Discuss your response with the Lord and thank him for his call in your life.

Record a summary of your discussion in section 4 and summarize your experience of the grace in section 5 in your journal.

In section 1 of your journal, record day, time, place, and condition.

Contemplatio: In section 2 of your journal, record your experience of the theme and grace since your last journal entry.

Meditatio: After repeating the theme several times, ask for the grace. Pausing for several minutes of silence between each reading, read Matthew 6:33 three times. Spend at least thirty minutes considering the invitation found in the Kingdom Exercise, Part Two (p. 180).

Oratio: Answer your King and thank him for his call in your life.

Record summaries of your meditation in section 3, your discussion in section 4, and your experience of the grace in section 5 in your journal.

Day **7** GRACE: Lord, open our hearts to trust your love.

In section 1 of your journal, record day, time, place, and condition.

Contemplatio: In section 2 of your journal, record your experience of the theme and grace since your last journal entry.

Meditatio: Review all six days by reading your journal before you meet with your listener. Prepare a brief written summary for your listener.

Oratio: Meet and share your summary with your listener. Discuss how the theme and grace for this unit are seen in your meditations. Pray together and thank God for blessing you.

After meeting with your listener, record any new insights in section 3 and your emotions in section 4 of your journal.

U N I T 12

▪ Preliminary Comments

The Kingdom Exercise calls us to follow and serve with our King. This week we begin to consider the difficulties of such discipleship. With the help of the Two Standards Exercise, we begin to see the value of knowing our sinful tendencies—and the persons who have played upon them—so as not to come under their sway again.[24]

It is helpful at this point in the Exercises to begin lengthening the time of silence between your reading of the Scripture passages. Give this time to the Holy Spirit and allow God to use the silence to transform your heart and mind.

Occasionally, sensitive persons are offended by the strong military imagery of this Ignatian parable. If this is the case for you, spend some time and rewrite it in images appropriate to your context. (Everyone is asked to do this at the end of unit 13.)

THEME: As I hear the Lord's call to serve with him, I also experience the tug of riches and honor.

GRACE: Lord Jesus, allow me to recognize and hate evil, and so follow only your will.[25]

In section 1 of your journal, record day, time, place, and Day **1** condition.

Contemplatio: In section 2 of your journal, briefly record your experience of God's love since you met with your listener.

Meditatio: After repeating the theme several times, ask for the grace. Pausing for several minutes of silence between each reading, read Ephesians 6:10–13 three times. Spend at least thirty minutes considering the Preparation and First Point of the Two Standards Exercise (p. 180).[26]

Oratio: Discuss your battle. Ask for grace to be true to your Lord.

Record summaries of your meditation in section 3, your discussion in section 4, and your experience of the grace in section 5 in your journal.

Day **2** In section 1 of your journal, record day, time, place, and condition.

Contemplatio: In section 2 of your journal, record your experience of the theme and grace since your last journal entry.

Meditatio: After repeating the theme several times, ask for the grace. Pausing for several minutes of silence between each reading, read Matthew 13:24–30, 36–43 three times. Spend at least thirty minutes considering the First Point of the Two Standards Exercise.

Oratio: Discuss this with the Lord and thank him for his call in your life.

Record summaries of your meditation in section 3, your discussion in section 4, and your experience of the grace in section 5 in your journal.

Day **3** In section 1 of your journal, record day, time, place, and condition.

Contemplatio: In section 2 of your journal, record your experience of the theme and grace since your last journal entry.

Meditatio: After repeating the theme several times, ask for the grace. Pausing for several minutes of silence between each reading, read Luke 18:18–30 three times. Spend at least thirty minutes considering the First Point of the Two Standards Exercise.

Oratio: Discuss this with the Lord and thank him for his call in your life.

Record summaries of your meditation in section 3, your discussion in section 4, and your experience of the grace in section 5 in your journal.

In section 1 of your journal, record day, time, place, and condition.

Contemplatio: In section 2 of your journal, record your experience of the theme and grace since your last journal entry.

Meditatio: After repeating the theme several times, ask for the grace. Pausing for several minutes of silence between each reading, read Mark 6:17–44 twice.[27] Spend at least thirty minutes considering these two feasts in light of the Second Point of the Two Standards (p. 180).

Oratio: Discuss this with the Lord and thank him for his call in your life.

Record summaries of your meditation in section 3, your discussion in section 4, and your experience of the grace in section 5 in your journal.

In section 1 of your journal, record day, time, place, and condition.

Contemplatio: In section 2 of your journal, record your experience of the theme and grace since your last journal entry.

Meditatio: After repeating the theme several times, ask for the grace. Pausing for several minutes of silence between each reading, read the ninth Rule for Discernment[28] (pp. 178–79) several times. Briefly record your meditation in section 3 of your journal.

Oratio: Ask, "Lord, how does this illumine my struggle to follow you?"

Record a summary of your discussion in section 4 and summarize your experience of the grace in section 5 in your journal.

Day 6 In section 1 of your journal, record day, time, place, and condition.

Contemplatio: In section 2 of your journal, record your experience of the theme and grace since your last journal entry.

Meditatio: After repeating the theme several times, ask for the grace. Pausing for several minutes of silence between each reading, read Matthew 13:44–46 three times. Briefly record your meditation in section 3 of your journal.

Oratio: Discuss this with the Lord and thank him for his call in your life.

Record a summary of your discussion in section 4 and summarize your experience of the grace in section 5 in your journal.

Day 7 GRACE: Lord, open our hearts to trust your love.

In section 1 of your journal, record day, time, place, and condition.

Contemplatio: In section 2 of your journal, record your experience of the theme and grace since your last journal entry.

Meditatio: Review all six days by reading your journal before you meet with your listener. Prepare a brief written summary for your listener.

Oratio: Meet and share your summary with your listener. Discuss how the theme and grace for this unit are seen in your meditations. Pray together and thank God for blessing you.

After meeting with your listener, record any new insights in section 3 and your emotions in section 4 of your journal.

Unit 13

■ Preliminary Comments

Christ called his disciples to a radically different kind of life. As we choose to follow Jesus, our enemy sometimes intensifies his attacks and sometimes withdraws, for he hopes that we will fall into some form of ease and neglect our spiritual exercises. In both instances, we should seek to draw closer to Christ.

You will want to plan some extra time for a more extensive review on day 7.

> **THEME:** In seeking to follow Jesus, I hope
> to trust God more than anything I am or possess.

GRACE: Jesus, allow me to recognize and hate evil, that I might follow only your will.

In section 1 of your journal, record day, time, place, and Day **1** condition.

Contemplatio: In section 2 of your journal, briefly record your experience of God's love since you met with your listener.

Meditatio: After repeating the theme several times, ask for the grace. Pausing for several minutes of silence between each reading, read Ephesians 6:13–17 three times. Spend at least thirty minutes considering it in light of the Second Point of the Two Standards (p. 180).

Oratio: Discuss your battle. Ask for grace to be true to your Lord.

Record summaries of your meditation in section 3, your discussion in section 4, and your experience of the grace in section 5 in your journal.

Day **2** In section 1 of your journal, record day, time, place, and condition.

Contemplatio: In section 2 of your journal, record your experience of the theme and grace since your last journal entry.

Meditatio: After repeating the theme several times, ask for the grace. Pausing for several minutes of silence between each reading, read Luke 5:1–11 three times.[29] Using all five senses, witness this second call of Peter in light of the Second Point of the Two Standards.

Oratio: Discuss this with the Lord and thank him for his call in your life.

Record summaries of your meditation in section 3, your discussion in section 4, and your experience of the grace in section 5 in your journal.

Day **3** In section 1 of your journal, record day, time, place, and condition.

Contemplatio: In section 2 of your journal, record your experience of the theme and grace since your last journal entry.

Meditatio: After repeating the theme several times, ask for the grace. Pausing for several minutes of silence between each reading, read 1 Corinthians 10:12–13 three times. Consider how this supports the tenth and eleventh Rules for Discernment (p. 179).[30]

Oratio: Discuss this with the Lord and thank him for his call in your life.

Record summaries of your meditation in section 3, your discussion in section 4, and your experience of the grace in section 5 in your journal.

Day **4** In section 1 of your journal, record day, time, place, and condition.

Contemplatio: In section 2 of your journal, record your experience of the theme and grace since your last journal entry.

Meditatio: After repeating the theme several times, ask for the grace. Pausing for several minutes of silence between each reading, read Matthew 23:1–14 three times. Consider this in terms of the Second Point of the Two Standards.

Oratio: Discuss this with the Lord and thank him for his call in your life.

Record summaries of your meditation in section 3, your discussion in section 4, and your experience of the grace in section 5 in your journal.

In section 1 of your journal, record day, time, place, and condition. Day **5**

Contemplatio: In section 2 of your journal, record your experience of the theme and grace since your last journal entry.

Meditatio: After repeating the theme several times, ask for the grace. Pausing for several minutes of silence between each reading, read Mark 1:21–27 three times. Using all five senses, witness this in terms of the Second Point of the Two Standards.

Oratio: Discuss this with the Lord and thank him for his call in your life.

Record summaries of your meditation in section 3, your discussion in section 4, and your experience of the grace in section 5 in your journal.

In section 1 of your journal, record day, time, place, and condition. Day **6**

Contemplatio: In section 2 of your journal, record your experience of the theme and grace since your last journal entry.

Meditatio: Rewrite the Two Standards in images and language appropriate to your context in life in section 3 of your journal.

Oratio: Discuss this with the Lord and answer the Third Point (p. 180).

Record a summary of your discussion in section 4 and summarize your experience of the grace in section 5 in your journal.

Day 7 **GRACE:** Lord, open our hearts to trust your love.

In section 1 of your journal, record day, time, place, and condition.

Contemplatio: In section 2 of your journal, record your experience of the theme and grace since your last journal entry.

Meditatio: Prayerfully review your journal for units 10–13. What do your responses reveal about the call of God in your life? Prepare a brief written summary for your listener. It may be helpful to again record your views of God, self, and the purpose of your life for units 10–13 on a summary chart.

Oratio: Meet and share your summary with your listener. Discuss how the theme and grace for this unit are seen in your meditations. Pray together and thank God for blessing you.

After meeting with your listener, record any new insights in section 3 and your emotions in section 4 of your journal.

UNIT 14

■ **Preliminary Comments**

Ignatius gives us a rather pointed tool for self-examination called the Three Classes of People. This meditation describes three types or "classes" of people in terms of how they use material possessions. There are, of course, many more than these three kinds and yet there is much to be gained by focusing on these three.

> **THEME:** God has given me many gifts
> and abilities for building up his kingdom.

GRACE: Lord, help me use my material possessions for your greater glory.[31]

In section 1 of your journal, record day, time, place, and ^Day **1** condition.

Contemplatio: In section 2 of your journal, briefly record your experience of God's love since you met with your listener.

Meditatio: After repeating the theme several times, ask for the grace. Pausing for several minutes of silence between each reading, read 1 Timothy 6:17–19 three times. In this first meditation on the Three Classes of People (p. 181), ask to understand what characterizes the first class of people.

Oratio: With the Lord, consider how you want to differ from them.

Record summaries of your meditation in section 3, your discussion in section 4, and your experience of the grace in section 5 in your journal.

Day 2 In section 1 of your journal, record day, time, place, and condition.

Contemplatio: In section 2 of your journal, record your experience of the theme and grace since your last journal entry.

Meditatio: After repeating the theme several times, ask for the grace. Pausing for several minutes of silence between each reading, read Matthew 7:21–23 three times.

Oratio: Discuss with the Lord when and how you are tempted to be like those described in Matthew 7:21–23.

Record summaries of your meditation in section 3, your discussion in section 4, and your experience of the grace in section 5 in your journal.

Day 3 In section 1 of your journal, record day, time, place, and condition.

Contemplatio: In section 2 of your journal, record your experience of the theme and grace since your last journal entry.

Meditatio: After repeating the theme several times, ask for the grace. Pausing for several minutes of silence between each reading, read Matthew 6:19–24 three times.

Oratio: Discuss with the Lord where you are tempted to become a slave to material things.

Record summaries of your meditation in section 3, your discussion in section 4, and your experience of the grace in section 5 in your journal.

Day 4 In section 1 of your journal, record day, time, place, and condition.

Contemplatio: In section 2 of your journal, record your experience of the theme and grace since your last journal entry.

Meditatio: After repeating the theme several times, ask for the grace. Again, read 1 Timothy 6:17–19 three times. Pause for several minutes of silence between each reading. Meditate upon the second class of people. What characterizes their life? How do you differ from them?

Oratio: With the Lord, consider how you want to differ from them.

Record summaries of your meditation in section 3, your discussion in section 4, and your experience of the grace in section 5 in your journal.

In section 1 of your journal, record day, time, place, and condition. **Day 5**

Contemplatio: In section 2 of your journal, record your experience of the theme and grace since your last journal entry.

Meditatio: After repeating the theme several times, ask for the grace. Pausing for several minutes of silence between each reading, read Mark 7:9–13 three times. What characterizes these leaders?

Oratio: With the Lord, consider how you want to differ from them.

Record summaries of your meditation in section 3, your discussion in section 4, and your experience of the grace in section 5 in your journal.

In section 1 of your journal, record day, time, place, and condition. **Day 6**

Contemplatio: In section 2 of your journal, record your experience of the theme and grace since your last journal entry.

Meditatio: After repeating the theme several times, ask for the grace. Pausing for several minutes of silence between each reading, read Luke 18:18–27 three times. What characterizes this man's life?

Oratio: With the Lord, consider how you want to differ from this man.

Record summaries of your meditation in section 3, your discussion in section 4, and your experience of the grace in section 5 in your journal.

Day **7** **GRACE:** Lord, open our hearts to trust your love.

In section 1 of your journal, record day, time, place, and condition.

Contemplatio: In section 2 of your journal, record your experience of the theme and grace since your last journal entry.

Meditatio: Review all six days by reading your journal before you meet with your listener. Prepare a brief written summary for your listener.

Oratio: Meet and share your summary with your listener. Discuss how the theme and grace for this unit are seen in your meditations. Pray together and thank God for blessing you.

After meeting with your listener, record any new insights in section 3 and your emotions in section 4 of your journal.

UNIT 15

■ **Preliminary Comments**

This unit continues to explore our involvement with the kingdom of God and calls us to a more responsible citizenship. We seek a practical understanding of the third class of people. We seek to understand the concept of indifference in the Principle and Foundation in practical and everyday terms.[32] Most simply put, we seek to give ourselves and our possessions to God in the most profound way.

> **THEME:** Jesus has given me many gifts
> and abilities for building up his kingdom.

GRACE: Lord, help me use my material possessions for your greater glory.

In section 1 of your journal, record day, time, place, and ^{Day} **1** condition.

Contemplatio: In section 2 of your journal, briefly record your experience of God's love since you met with your listener.

Meditatio: After repeating the theme several times, ask for the grace. Pausing for several minutes of silence between each reading, read 1 Timothy 6:17–19 three times and meditate on the strengths of the third class of people (p. 181).

Oratio: Discuss this with the Lord and thank him for the joy of sharing so many gifts.

Record summaries of your meditation in section 3, your discussion in section 4, and your experience of the grace in section 5 in your journal.

Day 2 In section 1 of your journal, record day, time, place, and condition.

Contemplatio: In section 2 of your journal, record your experience of the theme and grace since your last journal entry.

Meditatio: After repeating the theme several times, ask for the grace. Pausing for several minutes of silence between each reading, read Luke 19:1–10 three times and imagine that you are Zacchaeus. How is your life changing now that you have taken these bold steps?

Oratio: Discuss this with the Lord and thank him for the joy of sharing so many gifts.

Record summaries of your meditation in section 3, your discussion in section 4, and your experience of the grace in section 5 in your journal.

Day 3 In section 1 of your journal, record day, time, place, and condition.

Contemplatio: In section 2 of your journal, record your experience of the theme and grace since your last journal entry.

Meditatio: After repeating the theme several times, ask for the grace. Pausing for several minutes of silence between each reading, read James 4:7 and 1 Peter 5:8–9 and then meditate upon the twelfth Rule for Discernment (p. 179).[33] Consider how you can act opposite to temptation. For example, when tempted to be greedy, we give generously; or when tempted to be slothful, we renew our discipline. Briefly record your meditation in section 3 of your journal.

Oratio: Discuss your experience of temptation with the Lord and thank him for his great love for you.

Record a summary of your discussion in section 4 and summarize your experience of the grace in section 5 in your journal.

In section 1 of your journal, record day, time, place, and Day 4 condition.

Contemplatio: In section 2 of your journal, record your experience of the theme and grace since your last journal entry.

Meditatio: After repeating the theme several times, ask for the grace. Pausing for several minutes of silence between each reading, read Matthew 6:25–34 three times. How are you experiencing these promises?

Oratio: Discuss this with the Lord and thank him for the joy of sharing so many gifts.

Record summaries of your meditation in section 3, your discussion in section 4, and your experience of the grace in section 5 in your journal.

In section 1 of your journal, record day, time, place, and Day 5 condition.

Contemplatio: In section 2 of your journal, record your experience of the theme and grace since your last journal entry.

Meditatio: After repeating the theme several times, ask for the grace. Pausing for several minutes of silence between each reading, read Luke 10:25–37 three times and use all five senses as you witness the good Samaritan's actions.

Oratio: Discuss this with the Lord and thank him for the joy of sharing so many gifts.

Record summaries of your meditation in section 3, your discussion in section 4, and your experience of the grace in section 5 in your journal.

In section 1 of your journal, record day, time, place, and Day 6 condition.

Contemplatio: In section 2 of your journal, record your experience of the theme and grace since your last journal entry.

Meditatio: After repeating the theme several times, ask for the grace. Pausing for several minutes of silence between each reading, read James 5:16 and meditate upon the thirteenth Rule for Discernment (p. 179).[34] Briefly record your meditation in section 3 of your journal.

Oratio: Discuss this with the Lord and thank him for the joy of sharing so many gifts.

Record a summary of your discussion in section 4 and summarize your experience of the grace in section 5 in your journal.

Day **7** **GRACE:** Lord, open our hearts to trust your love.

In section 1 of your journal, record day, time, place, and condition.

Contemplatio: In section 2 of your journal, record your experience of the theme and grace since your last journal entry.

Meditatio: Review all six days by reading your journal before you meet with your listener. Prepare a brief written summary for your listener.

Oratio: Meet and share your summary with your listener. Discuss how the theme and grace for this unit are seen in your meditations. Pray together and thank God for blessing you.

After meeting with your listener, record any new insights in section 3 and your emotions in section 4 of your journal.

Unit 16

■ Preliminary Comments

Ignatius calls us to a still deeper examination of our lifestyle through the Three Kinds of Humility. Again, these are only representative of many "kinds" of humility.

You will want to plan some extra time for a more extensive review on day 7.

> **THEME:** Jesus desires that I serve with him
> in building up the kingdom of God.

GRACE: Lord, give me a desire to obey you in all things and, if it brings you greater glory, even to bear poverty and persecutions in your name.[35]

In section 1 of your journal, record day, time, place, and condition.

Day 1

Contemplatio: In section 2 of your journal, briefly record your experience of God's love since you met with your listener.

Meditatio: After repeating the theme several times, ask for the grace. Pausing for several minutes of silence between each reading, read Mark 10:42–45 three times.

Oratio: Discuss this with the Lord and thank him for his call in your life.

Record summaries of your meditation in section 3, your discussion in section 4, and your experience of the grace in section 5 in your journal.

In section 1 of your journal, record day, time, place, and condition.

Day 2

Contemplatio: In section 2 of your journal, record your experience of the theme and grace since your last journal entry.

Meditatio: After repeating the theme several times, ask for the grace. Pausing for several minutes of silence between each reading, read the Three Kinds of Humility three times (pp. 181–82). Consider the motives characteristic of the first kind of humility. Describe a time when you reacted this way.

Oratio: Discuss this with the Lord and thank him for his call in your life.

Record summaries of your meditation in section 3, your discussion in section 4, and your experience of the grace in section 5 in your journal.

Day **3** In section 1 of your journal, record day, time, place, and condition.

Contemplatio: In section 2 of your journal, record your experience of the theme and grace since your last journal entry.

Meditatio: After repeating the theme several times, ask for the grace. Pausing for several minutes of silence between each reading, read Luke 7:1–10 three times. Observe the centurion's opinion of himself and the opinion others had of him.

Oratio: Discuss this with the Lord and thank him for his call in your life.

Record summaries of your meditation in section 3, your discussion in section 4, and your experience of the grace in section 5 in your journal.

Day **4** In section 1 of your journal, record day, time, place, and condition.

Contemplatio: In section 2 of your journal, record your experience of the theme and grace since your last journal entry.

Meditatio: After repeating the theme several times, ask for the grace. Read the Three Kinds of Humility and consider the motives characteristic of the second kind of humility. Describe a time when you acted this way.

Oratio: Discuss this with the Lord and thank him for his call in your life.

Record summaries of your meditation in section 3, your discussion in section 4, and your experience of the grace in section 5 in your journal.

In section 1 of your journal, record day, time, place, and Day **5** condition.

Contemplatio: In section 2 of your journal, record your experience of the theme and grace since your last journal entry.

Meditatio: After repeating the theme several times, ask for the grace. Pausing for several minutes of silence between each reading, read Mark 12:41–44 three times. Witness this woman's generosity and Jesus's approval.

Oratio: Discuss this with the Lord and thank him for his call in your life.

Record summaries of your meditation in section 3, your discussion in section 4, and your experience of the grace in section 5 in your journal.

In section 1 of your journal, record day, time, place, and Day **6** condition.

Contemplatio: In section 2 of your journal, record your experience of the theme and grace since your last journal entry.

Meditatio: After repeating the theme several times, ask for the grace. Read the Three Kinds of Humility and consider the motives characteristic of the third kind of humility.

Oratio: Discuss this with the Lord and thank him for his call in your life.

Record summaries of your meditation in section 3, your discussion in section 4, and your experience of the grace in section 5 in your journal.

Day **7** GRACE: Lord, open our hearts to trust your love.

In section 1 of your journal, record day, time, place, and condition.

Contemplatio: In section 2 of your journal, record your experience of the theme and grace since your last journal entry.

Meditatio: Prayerfully review your journal for units 14–16. What do your responses reveal about the call of God in your life? Prepare a brief written summary for your listener. It may be helpful to again record your views of God, self, and the purpose of your life for units 14–16 on a summary chart (see p. 183).

Oratio: Meet and share your summary with your listener. Discuss how the theme and grace for this unit are seen in your meditations. Pray together and thank God for blessing you.

After meeting with your listener, record any new insights in section 3 and your emotions in section 4 of your journal.

Unit 17

■ Preliminary Comments

Experience has shown that we are especially slow in understanding the motives of persons with the Third Kind of Humility. We are comforted by the discovery that the second kind of humility describes a person genuinely living the life called forth by the Principle and Foundation. But is there a deeper joy in suffering for our Lord? Will his love call us and gift us with this too? We can ask these questions, but we cannot change ourselves, our motives, or our call. We can be eager for such gifts and be faithful in our present service until he chooses to gift and call us differently. With this unit we turn toward Jerusalem and the final week of our Lord's ministry.

THEME: Jesus leads us to Jerusalem.

GRACE: Lord, give me a desire to obey you in all things and, if it brings you greater glory, even to bear poverty and persecutions in your name.

In section 1 of your journal, record day, time, place, and Day **1** condition.

Contemplatio: In section 2 of your journal, briefly record your experience of God's love since you met with your listener.

Meditatio: After repeating the theme several times, ask for the grace. Review your meditations on the Principle and Foundation in unit 5. Repeat the exercise in unit 5 that was most helpful or most difficult for you.

Oratio: Discuss with the Lord how your perceptions and desires have changed.

Record summaries of your meditation in section 3, your discussion in section 4, and your experience of the grace in section 5 in your journal.

Day 2 In section 1 of your journal, record day, time, place, and condition.

Contemplatio: In section 2 of your journal, record your experience of the theme and grace since your last journal entry.

Meditatio: After repeating the theme several times, ask for the grace. Pausing for several minutes of silence between each reading, read Matthew 17:1–13 three times.[36] As James, witness the transfiguration. Briefly record your meditation in section 3 of your journal.

Oratio: Discuss this with the Lord and thank him for the joy of following him.

Record a summary of your discussion in section 4 and summarize your experience of the grace in section 5 in your journal.

Day 3 In section 1 of your journal, record day, time, place, and condition.

Contemplatio: In section 2 of your journal, record your experience of the theme and grace since your last journal entry.

Meditatio: After repeating the theme several times, ask for the grace. Pausing for several minutes of silence between each reading, read John 11:1–44 and witness the raising of Lazarus.[37] Briefly record your meditation in section 3 of your journal.

Oratio: Discuss this with the Lord and thank him for the joy of following him.

Record a summary of your discussion in section 4 and summarize your experience of the grace in section 5 in your journal.

In section 1 of your journal, record day, time, place, and ^{Day}**4** condition.

Contemplatio: In section 2 of your journal, record your experience of the theme and grace since your last journal entry.

Meditatio: After repeating the theme several times, ask for the grace. Pausing for several minutes of silence between each reading, read Matthew 21:1–11 three times.[38] Follow Jesus on foot as you witness the triumphal entry. What do you see, hear, smell, taste, and feel? Briefly record your meditation in section 3 of your journal.

Oratio: Discuss this with the Lord and thank him for the joy of following him.

Record a summary of your discussion in section 4 and summarize your experience of the grace in section 5 in your journal.

In section 1 of your journal, record day, time, place, and ^{Day}**5** condition.

Contemplatio: In section 2 of your journal, record your experience of the theme and grace since your last journal entry.

Meditatio: After repeating the theme several times, ask for the grace. Pausing for several minutes of silence between each reading, read Matthew 21:12–17 three times.[39] What do you see, hear, smell, taste, and feel during this "cleansing of the temple"? Briefly record your meditation in section 3 of your journal.

Oratio: Discuss this with the Lord and thank him for the joy of following him.

Record a summary of your discussion in section 4 and summarize your experience of the grace in section 5 in your journal.

In section 1 of your journal, record day, time, place, and ^{Day}**6** condition.

Contemplatio: In section 2 of your journal, record your experience of the theme and grace since your last journal entry.

Meditatio: After repeating the theme several times, ask for the grace. Pausing for several minutes of silence between each reading, read 2 Corinthians 12:7–10 three times. Consider what it means to follow Christ in difficult times and still suffer your many imperfections. Briefly record your meditation in section 3 of your journal.

Oratio: Discuss this with the Lord and thank him for the joy of following him.

Record a summary of your discussion in section 4 and summarize your experience of the grace in section 5 in your journal.

Day **7** **GRACE:** Lord, open our hearts to trust your love.

In section 1 of your journal, record day, time, place, and condition.

Contemplatio: In section 2 of your journal, record your experience of the theme and grace since your last journal entry.

Meditatio: Review all six days by reading your journal before you meet with your listener. Prepare a brief written summary for your listener.

Oratio: Meet and share your summary with your listener. Discuss how the theme and grace for this unit are seen in your meditations. Pray together and thank God for blessing you.

After meeting with your listener, record any new insights in section 3 and your emotions in section 4 of your journal.

Unit 18

■ **Preliminary Comments**

As we review our accomplishments and life, we can easily become oppressed by our insignificance. Here we see the Lord's patience demonstrated with his disciples, who just do not quite understand what is really happening. As with them, Christ looks far beyond our faults and sees our potential in his kingdom. In this unit we are called to see the patience of the Lord with people like us.

> **THEME:** Christ is patient with his disciples
> in the midst of growing adversity.

GRACE: Lord, give me deep confidence in your patience and love.

In section 1 of your journal, record day, time, place, and ^{Day} **1** condition.

Contemplatio: In section 2 of your journal, briefly record your experience of God's love since you met with your listener.

Meditatio: After repeating the theme several times, ask for the grace. Pausing for several minutes of silence between each reading, read Matthew 26:6–13 three times.[40] Witness this scene from the viewpoint of some unimportant slave. Describe the reactions of Jesus and his disciples.

Oratio: Discuss this with the Lord and thank him for his patience and love.

Record summaries of your meditation in section 3, your discussion in section 4, and your experience of the grace in section 5 in your journal.

Day 2 In section 1 of your journal, record day, time, place, and condition.

Contemplatio: In section 2 of your journal, record your experience of the theme and grace since your last journal entry.

Meditatio: After repeating the theme several times, ask for the grace. Pausing for several minutes of silence between each reading, read John 13:1–16 three times.[41] As an insignificant servant, witness how Jesus washes the feet of Peter, Judas, and the rest of the disciples.

Oratio: Discuss this with the Lord and thank him for his patience and love.

Record summaries of your meditation in section 3, your discussion in section 4, and your experience of the grace in section 5 in your journal.

Day 3 In section 1 of your journal, record day, time, place, and condition.

Contemplatio: In section 2 of your journal, record your experience of the theme and grace since your last journal entry.

Meditatio: After repeating the theme several times, ask for the grace. Pausing for several minutes of silence between each reading, read Matthew 26:17–26 three times.[42] As an insignificant servant, witness the preparations for the Passover meal and then the discussion with Judas.

Oratio: Discuss this with the Lord and thank him for his patience and love.

Record summaries of your meditation in section 3, your discussion in section 4, and your experience of the grace in section 5 in your journal.

Day 4 In section 1 of your journal, record day, time, place, and condition.

Contemplatio: In section 2 of your journal, record your experience of the theme and grace since your last journal entry.

Meditatio: After repeating the theme several times, ask for the grace. Pausing for several minutes of silence between each reading, read Matthew 26:26–30 three times.[43] As an insignificant servant, witness the Passover meal and the institution of the eucharistic meal or Lord's Supper.

Oratio: Discuss this with the Lord and thank him for his patience and love.

Record summaries of your meditation in section 3, your discussion in section 4, and your experience of the grace in section 5 in your journal.

In section 1 of your journal, record day, time, place, and **Day 5** condition.

Contemplatio: In section 2 of your journal, record your experience of the theme and grace since your last journal entry.

Meditatio: After repeating the theme several times, ask for the grace. Pausing for several minutes of silence between each reading, read Luke 22:24–31 three times. Witness this conversation and ask to see the Lord's patience with each of us. What is his call to you?

Oratio: Discuss this with the Lord and thank him for his patience and love.

Record summaries of your meditation in section 3, your discussion in section 4, and your experience of the grace in section 5 in your journal.

In section 1 of your journal, record day, time, place, and **Day 6** condition.

Contemplatio: In section 2 of your journal, record your experience of the theme and grace since your last journal entry.

Meditatio: After repeating the theme several times, ask for the grace. Meditate on the ninth Rule for Discernment (p. 178), and consider that the greatest temptation during desolation—indeed the whole purpose of the enemy in bringing desolation—is that we would choose to leave the spiritual life entirely. Briefly record your meditation in section 3 of your journal.

Oratio: Discuss this with the Lord and thank him for his call in your life.

Record a summary of your discussion in section 4 and summarize your experience of the grace in section 5 in your journal.

Day **7** GRACE: Lord, open our hearts to trust your love.

In section 1 of your journal, record day, time, place, and condition.

Contemplatio: In section 2 of your journal, record your experience of the theme and grace since your last journal entry.

Meditatio: Review all six days by reading your journal before you meet with your listener. Prepare a brief written summary for your listener.

Oratio: Meet and share your summary with your listener. Discuss how the theme and grace for this unit are seen in your meditations. After reading the Preliminary Comments to the following Decision-Making Unit, discuss the possibility of doing this unit with your listener. Pray together and thank God for blessing you.

After meeting with your listener, record any new insights in section 3 and your emotions in section 4 of your journal.

DECISION-MAKING UNIT (OPTIONAL)

▪ Preliminary Comments

Many disciples begin to question their past decisions as they meditate on the Three Classes of People and the Three Kinds of Humility. If you find yourself asking questions about your career choices, your possessions, and your future commitments, this may be a good time to reconsider some of these decisions. Reconsidering these decisions now allows them to be tested in light of the Passion.

If you are not asking such questions, it is not a sign of failure in any way. In this case it is entirely permissible to consider this Decision-Making Unit as optional, and move on to the third movement.

Ignatius gave us some wonderful tools for finding peace in decisions we need to make or change. It may be that you do not need to make any major changes now, and so this unit may lack intensity. We are not looking to cause discontent. In any case, this simplified method for making decisions is well worth learning.[44] As always, with important and life-changing decisions, you are urged to get good counsel from trusted friends and mentors.

THEME: As a disciple, I examine my life
to discover areas my Lord calls me to change.

GRACE: Christ, give me peace as I submit my decisions to your will.

In section 1 of your journal, record day, time, place, and ^{Day} **1** condition.

141

Contemplatio: In section 2 of your journal, briefly record your experience of God's love since you met with your listener.

Meditatio: After repeating the theme several times, ask for the grace. Pausing for several minutes of silence between each reading, read Psalm 37:3–7 three times. Review the first four Rules for Discernment. Are you experiencing consolation or desolation? If you are experiencing desolation, do not proceed with this decision-making unit. Wait until you are in consolation or in a time of quiet.

Oratio: Discuss this with the Lord and thank him for care and guidance.

Record summaries of your meditation in section 3, your discussion in section 4, and your experience of the grace in section 5 in your journal.

Day **2** In section 1 of your journal, record day, time, place, and condition.

Contemplatio: In section 2 of your journal, record your experience of the theme and grace since your last journal entry.

Meditatio: After repeating the theme several times, ask for the grace. Meditate on Matthew 6:33–34 and review the fifth and sixth Rules for Discernment. Consider the major decisions you have made in your life. Which of these were made in consolation? Which decisions were made in desolation?

Oratio: Discuss this with the Lord and thank him for his forgiveness and guidance.

Record summaries of your meditation in section 3, your discussion in section 4, and your experience of the grace in section 5 in your journal.

Day **3** In section 1 of your journal, record day, time, place, and condition.

Contemplatio: In section 2 of your journal, record your experience of the theme and grace since your last journal entry.

Meditatio: After repeating the theme several times, ask for the grace. Meditate on Matthew 6:9–13, and without dwelling upon unchangeable decisions (there is no permission here to leave a marriage or cease nurturing your children), nor upon decisions made in periods of consolation, which of the decisions considered in day 2 do you wish you could change? Ask Christ to help you discern which of these it might be nice to change, and which of these you truly want to change.

Oratio: Discuss this with the Lord and thank him for his forgiveness and guidance.

Record summaries of your meditation in section 3, your discussion in section 4, and your experience of the grace in section 5 in your journal.

In section 1 of your journal, record day, time, place, and Day **4** condition.

Contemplatio: In section 2 of your journal, record your experience of the theme and grace since your last journal entry.

Meditatio: After repeating the theme several times, ask for the grace. Again, meditate on Matthew 6:9–13 and pray this prayer. Decisions are best made one at a time. Rank those decisions you wish you could change in terms of importance to your life. Some choices cannot be changed immediately. For example, a change to a lower-paying, but more satisfying career is often hindered by our overextended budgets. In these cases, consider the steps that can be taken to come closer to the career change. For example, you may decide to simplify your lifestyle and pay off your bills. This opens many doors to the future.

Beginning with the most important decision, identify your options. Ask Christ to help you find indifference by not preferring any of the several options in and for themselves. Consider what you can do to bring him greater glory.

Oratio: Discuss this with the Lord and thank him for his forgiveness and guidance.

Record summaries of your meditation in section 3, your discussion in section 4, and your experience of the grace in section 5 in your journal.

Day 5 In section 1 of your journal, record day, time, place, and condition.

Contemplatio: In section 2 of your journal, record your experience of the theme and grace since your last journal entry.

Meditatio: After repeating the theme several times, ask for the grace. Meditate on the Lord's Prayer again, and then consider how Christ helps us find indifference as we objectify our various options. To do this, list as plainly as possible the advantages and disadvantages of each option in section 3 of your journal. Keep the Principle and Foundation in mind during this process. The Three Classes of People and Three Kinds of Humility are also helpful. As the advantage to Christ and his kingdom becomes clear, pray for peace in making and carrying out the best choice.

Oratio: Discuss this with the Lord and thank him for his forgiveness and guidance.

Record summaries of your discussion in section 4, and your experience of the grace in section 5 in your journal.

Day 6 In section 1 of your journal, record day, time, place, and condition.

Contemplatio: In section 2 of your journal, record your experience of the theme and grace since your last journal entry.

Meditatio: After repeating the theme several times, ask for the grace. Meditate on Philippians 4:6–7. The consolation we seek in making a decision does not mean feeling good at a superficial level or a lack of conflict. Often the decision we have made will bring us into conflict with authoritative structures, systems, and personalities. Christ calls us to inward peace, even when chaos boils around us. We continue to pray for firmness in our resolve to follow Christ and ask to desire his approval alone.

Oratio: Discuss this with the Lord and thank him for his forgiveness and guidance.

Record summaries of your meditation in section 3, your discussion in section 4, and your experience of the grace in section 5 in your journal.

GRACE: Lord, open our hearts to trust your love.   Day **7**

In section 1 of your journal, record day, time, place, and condition.

Contemplatio: In section 2 of your journal, record your experience of the theme and grace since your last journal entry.

Meditatio: Review all six days by reading your journal before you meet with your listener. Prepare a brief written summary for your listener.

Oratio: Meet and share your summary with your listener. Discuss any decisions you have made. Pray together and ask for guidance about others you might seek counsel from. Thank God for blessing you.

After meeting with your listener, record any new insights in section 3 and your emotions in section 4 of your journal.

The
Third
Movement

UNIT 19

■ **Preliminary Comments**

Unit 19 begins the third Ignatian Movement. If you are following the liturgical seasons, it makes good sense to pause at this point until two or three weeks before Easter. You may find great consolation in repeating some of the previous exercises. Discuss with your listener whether you should use your time to repeat the meditations giving you deepest consolation or those you found most difficult.

The suffering of Jesus is not something we like to think about. Yet it is central to the Gospels, occupying over one-quarter of the total space. Our purpose is not to feel miserable. Here we ask to taste the suffering of Christ and so better accept his love. In considering the arrest and trials of Jesus, focus upon his responses and reactions. See how they model the indifference of the Principle and Foundation.

THEME: Jesus suffered during his arrest and trials.

GRACE: Jesus, let me feel your sorrow, tears, and deep grief.

Day **1** In section 1 of your journal, record day, time, place, and condition.

Contemplatio: In section 2 of your journal, briefly record your experience of God's love since you met with your listener.

Meditatio: After repeating the theme several times, ask for the grace. Pausing for several minutes of silence between each reading, read Matthew 26:31–35 three times. Witness Jesus predict that all of his disciples will fall away.

Oratio: Discuss this with the Lord and thank him for suffering for you.

Record summaries of your meditation in section 3, your discussion in section 4, and your experience of the grace in section 5 in your journal.

In section 1 of your journal, record day, time, place, and ^{Day}**2** condition.

Contemplatio: In section 2 of your journal, record your experience of the theme and grace since your last journal entry.

Meditatio: After repeating the theme several times, ask for the grace. Pausing for several minutes of silence between each reading, read John 17:20–26 three times. Consider how Jesus prays for us to know his Father's love.

Oratio: Discuss this with the Lord and thank him for suffering for you.

Record summaries of your meditation in section 3, your discussion in section 4, and your experience of the grace in section 5 in your journal.

In section 1 of your journal, record day, time, place, and ^{Day}**3** condition.

Contemplatio: In section 2 of your journal, record your experience of the theme and grace since your last journal entry.

Meditatio: After repeating the theme several times, ask for the grace. Pausing for several minutes of silence between each reading, read Matthew 26:36–46 three times and witness Jesus's prayer in the Garden of Gethsemane with all five senses.[1]

Oratio: Discuss this with the Lord and thank him for suffering for you.

Record summaries of your meditation in section 3, your discussion in section 4, and your experience of the grace in section 5 in your journal.

Day 4 In section 1 of your journal, record day, time, place, and condition.

Contemplatio: In section 2 of your journal, record your experience of the theme and grace since your last journal entry.

Meditatio: After repeating the theme several times, ask for the grace. Pausing for several minutes of silence between each reading, read Matthew 26:47–56 three times.[2] Witness his arrest with all five senses.

Oratio: Discuss this with the Lord and thank him for suffering for you.

Record summaries of your meditation in section 3, your discussion in section 4, and your experience of the grace in section 5 in your journal.

Day 5 In section 1 of your journal, record day, time, place, and condition.

Contemplatio: In section 2 of your journal, record your experience of the theme and grace since your last journal entry.

Meditatio: After repeating the theme several times, ask for the grace. Pausing for several minutes of silence between each reading, read Matthew 26:57–68 three times. Witness the night session before the High Council from the viewpoint of the high priest's slave.

Oratio: Discuss this with the Lord and thank him for suffering for you.

Record summaries of your meditation in section 3, your discussion in section 4, and your experience of the grace in section 5 in your journal.

Day 6 In section 1 of your journal, record day, time, place, and condition.

Contemplatio: In section 2 of your journal, record your experience of the theme and grace since your last journal entry.

Meditatio: After repeating the theme several times, ask for the grace. Pausing for several minutes of silence between each reading, read Matthew 26:69–75 three times.[3] Witness Peter's denial with all five senses.

Oratio: Discuss this with the Lord and thank him for suffering for you.

Record summaries of your meditation in section 3, your discussion in section 4, and your experience of the grace in section 5 in your journal.

GRACE: Lord, open our hearts to trust your love.   Day **7**

In section 1 of your journal, record day, time, place, and condition.

Contemplatio: In section 2 of your journal, record your experience of the theme and grace since your last journal entry.

Meditatio: Review all six days by reading your journal before you meet with your listener. Prepare a brief written summary for your listener.

Oratio: Meet and share your summary with your listener. Discuss how the theme and grace for this unit are seen in your meditations. Pray together and thank God for blessing you.

After meeting with your listener, record any new insights in section 3 and your emotions in section 4 of your journal.

UNIT 20

■ **Preliminary Comments**

It is difficult for many of us to contemplate the passion of Christ. Here we want to observe the passion of the Lord with renewed vision. In many ways, we have become detached from suffering in the world and therefore from Christ.[4] We seek to take that which is well known and sit with it in silence. Let it draw you deeper into its mystery. Speak with the Lord only after prolonged silence.

You will want to plan some extra time for a more extensive review on day 7.

THEME: Jesus became suffering incarnate.

GRACE: Lord, teach me that your suffering was for me.

Day 1 In section 1 of your journal, record day, time, place, and condition.

Contemplatio: In section 2 of your journal, briefly record your experience of God's love since you met with your listener.

Meditatio: After repeating the theme several times, ask for the grace. Pausing for several minutes of silence between each reading, read Matthew 27:11–31[5] three times. Sit in silence for an extended period of time.

Oratio: Discuss this with the Lord and thank him for suffering for you.

Record summaries of your meditation in section 3, your discussion in section 4, and your experience of the grace in section 5 in your journal.

In section 1 of your journal, record day, time, place, and ^{Day}**2** condition.

Contemplatio: In section 2 of your journal, record your experience of the theme and grace since your last journal entry.

Meditatio: After repeating the theme several times, ask for the grace. Pausing for several minutes of silence between each reading, read Matthew 27:32–44.[6] Sit in silence for an extended period of time.

Oratio: Discuss this with the Lord and thank him for suffering for you.

Record summaries of your meditation in section 3, your discussion in section 4, and your experience of the grace in section 5 in your journal.

In section 1 of your journal, record day, time, place, and ^{Day}**3** condition.

Contemplatio: In section 2 of your journal, briefly record your experience of God's love since your last journal entry.

Meditatio: After repeating the theme several times, ask for the grace. Pausing for several minutes of silence between each reading, read Matthew 27:45–56.[7] Sit in silence for an extended period of time.

Oratio: Discuss this with the Lord and thank him for suffering for you.

Record summaries of your meditation in section 3, your discussion in section 4, and your experience of the grace in section 5 in your journal.

In section 1 of your journal, record day, time, place, and ^{Day}**4** condition.

Contemplatio: In section 2 of your journal, record your experience of the theme and grace since your last journal entry.

Meditatio: After repeating the theme several times, ask for the grace. Contemplate the crucifixion. (It may be helpful to sit or kneel before a crucifix, a cross, or even a painting of the crucifixion.) Be drawn into the suffering, as Christ calls out, "My God, my God, why have you forsaken me?" Sit in silence for an extended period of time.

Oratio: Discuss this with the Lord and thank him for suffering for you.

Record summaries of your meditation in section 3, your discussion in section 4, and your experience of the grace in section 5 in your journal.

Day **5** In section 1 of your journal, record day, time, place, and condition.

Contemplatio: In section 2 of your journal, record your experience of the theme and grace since your last journal entry.

Meditatio: After repeating the theme several times, ask for the grace. Pausing for several minutes of silence between each reading, read Matthew 27:57–66.[8] Sit in silence for an extended period of time.

Oratio: Discuss this with the Lord and thank him for suffering for you.

Record summaries of your meditation in section 3, your discussion in section 4, and your experience of the grace in section 5 in your journal.

Day **6** In section 1 of your journal, record day, time, place, and condition.

Contemplatio: In section 2 of your journal, record your experience of the theme and grace since your last journal entry.

Meditatio: After repeating the theme several times, ask for the grace. Pausing for several minutes of silence between each reading, read 2 Corinthians 5:17 three times. Sit in silence for an extended period of time.

Oratio: Discuss this with the Lord and thank him for suffering for you.

Record summaries of your meditation in section 3, your discussion in section 4, and your experience of the grace in section 5 in your journal.

GRACE: Lord, open our hearts to trust your love.

In section 1 of your journal, record day, time, place, and condition.

Contemplatio: In section 2 of your journal, record your experience of the theme and grace since your last journal entry.

Meditatio: Prayerfully review your journal for units 17–20. What do your responses reveal about the call of God in your life? Prepare a brief written summary for your listener. It may be helpful to again chart your views of God, self, and the purpose of your life for units 17–20 on a summary chart.

Oratio: Meet and share your summary with your listener. Discuss how the theme and grace for this unit are seen in your meditations. Pray together and thank God for blessing you.

After meeting with your listener, record any new insights in section 3 and your emotions in section 4 of your journal.

THE
FOURTH
MOVEMENT

UNIT 21

■ **Preliminary Comments**

We are so quick in rushing into Easter that we do not appreciate the astonishment of Christ's first disciples. For us, the resurrection is at worst an intellectual problem that we cannot fully explain. For them, it was an impossibility. Some of them had touched his corpse. To the extent that we have contemplated his suffering and death, we will find interior joy in contemplating his resurrection.

> **THEME:** Jesus restores his disciples' faith and hope.

Day **1** **GRACE:** Ask to feel the disciples' astonishment, wonder, and fear.

In section 1 of your journal, record day, time, place, and condition.

Contemplatio: In section 2 of your journal, briefly record your experience of God's love since you met with your listener.

Meditatio: After repeating the theme several times, ask for the grace. Pausing for several minutes of silence between each reading, read Mark 16:1–8 three times.

Oratio: Discuss this with the Lord and thank him for his resurrection.

Record summaries of your meditation in section 3, your discussion in section 4, and your experience of the grace in section 5 in your journal.

Day **2** **GRACE:** Ask to feel the disciples' confusion and pain.

In section 1 of your journal, record day, time, place, and condition.

Contemplatio: In section 2 of your journal, record your experience of the disciples' astonishment, wonder, and fear.

Meditatio: After repeating the theme several times, ask for the grace. Pausing for several minutes of silence between each reading, read John 20:1–10 three times.

Oratio: Discuss this with the Lord and thank him for his call in your life.

Record summaries of your meditation in section 3, your discussion in section 4, and your experience of the grace in section 5 in your journal.

GRACE: Ask the Holy Spirit to transform your sorrow into Day **3** deep interior joy.

In section 1 of your journal, record day, time, place, and condition.

Contemplatio: In section 2 of your journal, record your experience of the disciples' confusion and pain.

Meditatio: After repeating the theme several times, ask for the grace. Pausing for several minutes of silence between each reading, read John 20:11–18 three times.

Oratio: Discuss this with the Lord and thank him for his call in your life.

Record summaries of your meditation in section 3, your discussion in section 4, and your experience of the grace in section 5 in your journal.

GRACE: Ask the risen Christ to overcome your spiritual Day **4** blindness.

In section 1 of your journal, record day, time, place, and condition.

Contemplatio: In section 2 of your journal, record your experience of the ongoing transformation of your sorrow into deep interior joy.

Meditatio: After repeating the theme several times, ask for the grace. Pausing for several minutes of silence between each reading, read Luke 24:13–33 three times.

Oratio: Discuss this with the Lord and thank him for his call in your life.

Record summaries of your meditation in section 3, your discussion in section 4, and your experience of the grace in section 5 in your journal.

Day **5** **GRACE:** Ask the risen Christ to renew your faith.

In section 1 of your journal, record day, time, place, and condition.

Contemplatio: In section 2 of your journal, record your ongoing experience of renewed spiritual sight.

Meditatio: After repeating the theme several times, ask for the grace. Pausing for several minutes of silence between each reading, read John 20:24–29 three times. It may be helpful to consider Thomas's previous deep commitment (John 11:16) as you ask the risen Christ to renew your faith.

Oratio: Discuss this with the Lord and thank him for his call in your life.

Record summaries of your meditation in section 3, your discussion in section 4, and your experience of the grace in section 5 in your journal.

Day **6** **GRACE:** Ask the risen Christ to let you receive forgiveness for your denials.

In section 1 of your journal, record day, time, place, and condition.

Contemplatio: In section 2 of your journal, record your ongoing experience of renewed faith.

Meditatio: After repeating the theme several times, ask for the grace. Pausing for several minutes of silence between each reading, read John 21:1–17 three times.

Oratio: Discuss this with the Lord and thank him for his call in your life.

Record summaries of your meditation in section 3, your discussion in section 4, and your experience of the grace in section 5 in your journal.

GRACE: Lord, open our hearts to trust your love. Day **7**

In section 1 of your journal, record day, time, place, and condition.

Contemplatio: In section 2 of your journal, record your on-going experience of receiving forgiveness for your denials.

Meditatio: Review all six days by reading your journal before you meet with your listener. Prepare a brief written summary for your listener.

Oratio: Meet and share your summary with your listener. Discuss how the theme and grace for this unit are seen in your meditations. Pray together and thank God for blessing you.

After meeting with your listener, record any new insights in section 3 and your emotions in section 4 of your journal.

Unit 22

Preliminary Comments

At this point in the Exercises, many disciples experience an odd phenomenon: they encounter a significant dry spell. They feel as though all consolation has left them, and they are somewhat numb. Many simply lay the Exercises aside at this point and go on with life. After several weeks (or even months) of these doldrums, they are roused and begin to see that the Lord has indeed shaped many of their perceptions and values through the Exercises. This experience of numbness is so common that we should take a few moments to understand it.

For many disciples, this numbness (or even mild depression) is a natural consequence of enduring a rather intense and emotional period. When the Exercises are coupled with the liturgical cycle, so that the last several weeks correspond to Holy Week and Easter, this is often all the explanation we need. It may be appropriate at this point to take a couple days off and simply rest. Come back to the Exercises when you feel refreshed.

Others discover that this numbness is the beginning of a significant period of training, in which the Lord wants to teach them the second or third element of the ninth Rule for Discernment (page 178). When this is the case, it is critical that you continue to pray with the assignments and persevere for the love of Christ alone. Some deserts must be obediently endured and crossed. Listen to the silence, and seek to love Christ for his own sake. Your relationship with him is more important than the gifts he gives you.

For a few disciples, this numbness is an indication that they feel crushed by God's nearness.[1] If this is the case for you, please stay with the Exercises and get some sensitive pastoral care. You will profit a great deal by working with a trained spiritual director.

In almost all cases, we must admit that we are somewhat intimidated by the prospect of following the example of the apostle Paul in Philippians 3:7–11. Unit 22 invites us to enter this quest with him. Once again, we return to the Principle and Foundation.

THEME: The risen Christ calls me
to be filled with his love.

GRACE: Jesus, give me deeper love for you and for all your creation.

In section 1 of your journal, record day, time, place, and Day **1** condition.

Contemplatio: In section 2 of your journal, briefly record your experience of God's love since you met with your listener.

Meditatio: After repeating the theme several times, ask for the grace. Pausing for several minutes of silence between each reading, read Philippians 3:7–11 three times.

Oratio: Discuss your expectations, thoughts, and fears with the Lord. Thank him for loving you.

Record summaries of your meditation in section 3, your discussion in section 4, and your experience of the grace in section 5 in your journal.

In section 1 of your journal, record day, time, place, and Day **2** condition.

Contemplatio: In section 2 of your journal, record your experience of the theme and grace since your last journal entry.

Meditatio: After repeating the theme several times, ask for the grace. Pausing for several minutes of silence between each reading, read the Principle and Foundation several times.

Oratio: Discuss your expectations, thoughts, and fears with the Lord. Thank him for loving you.

Record summaries of your meditation in section 3, your discussion in section 4, and your experience of the grace in section 5 in your journal.

Day **3** In section 1 of your journal, record day, time, place, and condition.

Contemplatio: In section 2 of your journal, record your experience of the theme and grace since your last journal entry.

Meditatio: After repeating the theme several times, ask for the grace. Reflect upon Romans 2:4, and then ask the Lord to guide your thoughts as you begin to think about your future. Consider ways to demonstrate your love. Briefly record your meditation in section 3 of your journal.

Oratio: Discuss this with the Lord and thank him for loving you.

Record a summary of your discussion in section 4 and summarize your experience of the grace in section 5 in your journal.

Day **4** In section 1 of your journal, record day, time, place, and condition.

Contemplatio: In section 2 of your journal, record your experience of the theme and grace since your last journal entry.

Meditatio: After repeating the theme several times, ask for the grace. Pausing for several minutes of silence between each reading, read James 1:17 several times. Think of the many gifts you have received from God. How have you responded to these many graces? Briefly record your meditation in section 3 of your journal.

Oratio: Reply now to Christ in this way:

Take, Lord, and receive all my liberty, my memory, my intellect, and all my will—all that I have and possess. You gave them to me: to you, Lord, I return them. All is yours, dispose of all according to your will. Give me only your love and grace, for these are enough for me.[2]

Record a summary of your discussion in section 4 and summarize your experience of the grace in section 5 in your journal.

In section 1 of your journal, record day, time, place, and **Day 5** condition.

Contemplatio: In section 2 of your journal, record your experience of the theme and grace since your last journal entry.

Meditatio: After repeating the theme several times, ask for the grace. Pausing for several minutes of silence between each reading, read Acts 17:24–28a several times. Recall again the gifts God has given to humanity in general and to you in particular. You may do this Exercise in a field, forest, desert, or other outside place. Use all five senses.

Oratio: Respond to Christ by paraphrasing "Take, Lord." Discuss this with the Lord.

Record summaries of your meditation in section 3, your discussion in section 4, and your experience of the grace in section 5 in your journal.

In section 1 of your journal, record day, time, place, and **Day 6** condition.

Contemplatio: In section 2 of your journal, record your experience of the theme and grace since your last journal entry.

Meditatio: After repeating the theme several times, ask for the grace. Pausing for several minutes of silence between each reading, read Colossians 1:13–20 three times.

Oratio: Discuss this with the Lord and thank him for his call in your life.

Record summaries of your meditation in section 3, your discussion in section 4, and your experience of the grace in section 5 in your journal.

Day **7** **GRACE:** Lord, open our hearts to trust your love.

In section 1 of your journal, record day, time, place, and condition.

Contemplatio: In section 2 of your journal, record your experience of the theme and grace since your last journal entry.

Meditatio: Review all six days by reading your journal before you meet with your listener. Prepare a brief written summary for your listener.

Oratio: Meet and share your summary with your listener. Discuss how the theme and grace for this unit are seen in your meditations. Pray together and thank God for blessing you.

After meeting with your listener, record any new insights in section 3 and your emotions in section 4 of your journal.

Unit 23

■ Preliminary Comments

Time spent in these meditations changes the way we want to live. As we change, we become more useful to Christ and his kingdom. We conclude these Exercises by asking how Christ will use us.

You will want to plan some extra time for a more extensive review on day 7.

> **THEME:** Christ calls me to serve him
> by serving others.

GRACE: Lord Jesus, give me joy in serving you through others.

In section 1 of your journal, record day, time, place, and ^{Day}**1** condition.

Contemplatio: In section 2 of your journal, briefly record your experience of God's love since you met with your listener.

Meditatio: After repeating the theme several times, ask for the grace. Pausing for several minutes of silence between each reading, read John 15:1–8.

Oratio: Discuss this with the Lord and thank him for the call to fruitful service.

Record summaries of your meditation in section 3, your discussion in section 4, and your experience of the grace in section 5 in your journal.

In section 1 of your journal, record day, time, place, and ^{Day}**2** condition.

Contemplatio: In section 2 of your journal, record your experience of the theme and grace since your last journal entry.

Meditatio: After repeating the theme several times, ask for the grace. Pausing for several minutes of silence between each reading, read John 15:9–17 three times. Briefly record your meditation in section 3 of your journal.

Oratio: Discuss this with the Lord and thank him for the call to fruitful service.

Record a summary of your discussion in section 4 and summarize your experience of the grace in section 5 in your journal.

Day **3** In section 1 of your journal, record day, time, place, and condition.

Contemplatio: In section 2 of your journal, record your experience of the theme and grace since your last journal entry.

Meditatio: After repeating the theme several times, ask for the grace. Pausing for several minutes of silence between each reading, read Luke 19:11–27 three times. Briefly record your meditation in section 3 of your journal.

Oratio: Discuss this with the Lord and thank him for the call to fruitful service.

Record a summary of your discussion in section 4 and summarize your experience of the grace in section 5 in your journal.

Day **4** In section 1 of your journal, record day, time, place, and condition.

Contemplatio: In section 2 of your journal, record your experience of the theme and grace since your last journal entry.

Meditatio: After repeating the theme several times, ask for the grace. Consider again the Three Kinds of Humility. Contemplate your future as you ask again for the grace.

Oratio: Respond to the Lord with the prayer "Take, Lord":

Take, Lord, and receive all my liberty, my memory, my intellect, and all my will—all that I have and possess. You gave them to me: to you, Lord, I return them. All is yours, dispose of all according to your will. Give me only your love and grace, for these are enough for me.

Record a summary of your discussion in section 4 and summarize your experience of the grace in section 5 in your journal.

In section 1 of your journal, record day, time, place, and condition.   Day **5**

Contemplatio: In section 2 of your journal, record your experience of the theme and grace since your last journal entry.

Meditatio: After repeating the theme several times, ask for the grace. Pausing for several minutes of silence between each reading, read Matthew 25:31–46 three times. Briefly record your meditation in section 3 of your journal.

Oratio: Discuss this with the Lord and thank him for the joy of serving him.

Record a summary of your discussion in section 4 and summarize your experience of the grace in section 5 in your journal.

In section 1 of your journal, record day, time, place, and condition.   Day **6**

Contemplatio: In section 2 of your journal, record your experience of the theme and grace since your last journal entry.

Meditatio: After repeating the theme several times, ask for the grace. Pausing for several minutes of silence between each reading, read 2 Corinthians 12:7–10. Once again, ask Christ how he can use your weakness if you are filled with his love. Briefly record your meditation in section 3 of your journal.

Oratio: Discuss this with the Lord and thank him for the joy of serving him.

Record a summary of your discussion in section 4 and summarize your experience of the grace in section 5 in your journal.

Day **7** GRACE: Lord, open our hearts to trust your love.

In section 1 of your journal, record day, time, place, and condition.

Contemplatio: In section 2 of your journal, record your experience of the theme and grace since your last journal entry.

Meditatio: Prayerfully review your journal for units 21–23. What do your responses reveal about the call of God in your life? Prepare a brief written summary for your listener. It may be helpful to again record your views of God, self, and the purpose of your life for units 21–23 on a summary chart.

Oratio: Meet and share your summary with your listener. Discuss how the theme and grace for this unit are seen in your meditations. Pray together and thank God for blessing you.

After meeting with your listener, record any new insights in section 3 and your emotions in section 4 of your journal.

UNIT 24

▪ Preliminary Comments

These Exercises have occupied you for some time. It is hoped that you have been encouraged to grow mightily in respect to salvation. Our lives are pilgrimages—we are on an exciting journey together. Let us go forward with Christ!

In preparation for this continuing journey, *you will now want to start expanding section 2 in your journal.* During this last unit, spend at least fifteen minutes reviewing your life since your last journal entry. Ask the Holy Spirit to help you notice God's kindness. Thank God for all the good things you have received. Ask the Holy Spirit to help you see where you have failed to honor God's love. Confess these failures as sin and ask Jesus to help you change for his greater glory.[3] Let this become a daily discipline, and it will carry you far beyond these Exercises.

THEME: Christ calls me to
go on with him in joyful service.

GRACE: Lord, give me your peace as I expectantly consider the future.

In section 1 of your journal, record day, time, place, and Day **1** condition.

Contemplatio: As described above, spend at least fifteen minutes considering your experience of God's love since you met with your listener. Briefly record this in section 2 of your journal.

Meditatio: After repeating the theme several times, ask for the grace. Pausing for several minutes of silence between each reading, read Hebrews 9:11–15 three times.

Oratio: Discuss this with the Lord and thank him for the call to serve the living God.

Record summaries of your meditation in section 3, your discussion in section 4, and your experience of the grace in section 5 in your journal.

Day 2 In section 1 of your journal, record day, time, place, and condition.

Contemplatio: As described above, spend at least fifteen minutes considering your experience of God's love since you met with your listener. Briefly record this in section 2 of your journal.

Meditatio: After repeating the theme several times, ask for the grace. Read 2 Corinthians 10:3–5 and meditate on the fourteenth Rule for Discernment (p. 179).[4]

Oratio: Ask the Holy Spirit to make you wise in recognizing and resisting the enemy's advances. Discuss this with the Lord and thank him for his call in your life.

Record summaries of your meditation in section 3, your discussion in section 4, and your experience of the grace in section 5 in your journal.*

Day 3 In section 1 of your journal, record day, time, place, and condition.

Contemplatio: As described above, spend at least fifteen minutes considering your experience of God's love since you met with your listener. Briefly record this in section 2 of your journal.

Meditatio: After repeating the theme several times, ask for the grace. Pausing for several minutes of silence between each reading, read Colossians 3:12–17 three times. With your imagination consider what the church would be like if we

---

*Note: As you go on with the Lord, you will find it very helpful to meditate on the second set of Rules for Discerning Spirits. These caution us against how the enemy attacks us with false consolations. See Thomas Green, S.J., *Weeds among the Wheat* (Notre Dame, IN: Ave Maria Press, 1984) for an excellent introduction to these rules.

took these words seriously. Try to use all five senses. Briefly record your meditation in section 3 of your journal.

Oratio: Discuss this with the Lord and thank him for his call to live in community with other disciples.

Record a summary of your discussion in section 4 and summarize your experience of the grace in section 5 in your journal.

In section 1 of your journal, record day, time, place, and Day **4** condition.

Contemplatio: As described above, spend at least fifteen minutes considering your experience of God's love since you met with your listener. Briefly record this in section 2 of your journal.

Meditatio: After repeating the theme several times, ask for the grace. Pausing for several minutes of silence between each reading, read Philippians 4:4–9 three times.

Oratio: Discuss this with the Lord and thank him for the peace of God that passes all understanding.

Record summaries of your meditation in section 3, your discussion in section 4, and your experience of the grace in section 5 in your journal.

In section 1 of your journal, record day, time, place, and Day **5** condition.

Contemplatio: As described above, spend at least fifteen minutes considering your experience of God's love since you met with your listener. Briefly record this in section 2 of your journal.

Meditatio: After repeating the theme several times, ask for the grace. Pausing for several minutes of silence between each reading, read Hebrews 12:28–29 three times.

Oratio: Summarize your response as you pray "Take, Lord" (p. 182). Discuss this with the Lord.

Record summaries of your meditation in section 3, your discussion in section 4, and your experience of the grace in section 5 in your journal.

Day **6** In section 1 of your journal, record day, time, place, and condition.

Contemplatio: As described above, spend at least fifteen minutes considering your experience of God's love since you met with your listener. Briefly record this in section 2 of your journal.

Meditatio: After repeating the theme several times, ask for the grace. Pausing for several minutes of silence between each reading, read Revelation 22:1–5. In section 3 of your journal, consider: what is your future in Christ?

Oratio: Discuss this with the Lord and thank him for his call to joyful service.

Record summaries of your discussion in section 4 and your experience of the grace in section 5 in your journal.

Day **7** GRACE: Lord, open our hearts to trust your love.

In section 1 of your journal, record day, time, place, and condition.

Contemplatio: As described above, spend at least fifteen minutes considering your experience of God's love since you met with your listener. Briefly record this in section 2 of your journal.

Meditatio: Review all six days by reading your journal before you meet with your listener. Prepare a brief written summary for your listener.

Oratio: Meet and share your summary with your listener. Discuss how the theme and grace for this unit are seen in your meditations. Pray together and thank God for blessing you.

After meeting with your listener, record any new insights in section 3 and your emotions in section 4 of your journal.

Summary Comments

These Exercises provide a sure foundation for a vigorous spiritual life. You have made a good beginning. Where should you go from here? Please allow me to offer a few suggestions.

First, *meditatio!* Continue to listen to Christ speak through the Scriptures. Almost every narrative passage can be imaginatively considered, but start with the Gospel of Mark. Use a Bible like the NIV that gives paragraph headings, and meditate on a paragraph a day. You have had a good taste of meditating on the Epistles as you have prayed with parts of Philippians. Again, using the paragraphs in a Bible like the NIV, ask the Holy Spirit to deepen your understanding as you pray your way through the entire letter.

Second, *oratio!* Learn to pray with the Psalms. As the prayer book Jesus used, the Psalms have much to teach us about our life with Christ. Here are the words we long for as we seek to adore the Lord of all creation. Many of the prayers in the New Testament Epistles are also rich for meditation and imitation. Again, they teach us more about the will of God and encourage our souls. The prayer below (Eph. 3:14–21) is a fine place to start. And simple as it may seem, the Lord's Prayer is still the bedrock of our verbal response to our loving Father.

Third, *contemplatio!* By now, taking time to review your day with the Lord should be part of your routine. Every day, spend at least fifteen minutes reviewing your life. Ask the Holy Spirit to help you notice God's kindness. Thank God for all the good things you have received. Ask the Holy Spirit to help you see where you have failed to honor God's love. Confess these failures as sin and ask the Lord to help you change for his greater glory. Continue to use your journal and watch how the Holy Spirit uses Scripture to "read" you. This is the very heart of our lifelong *contemplatio*.

Fourth, *consider serving as a listener for others in a* Sacred Listening *program*. There is a great need for this in many congregations. You may even discover a ministry of listening.

Fifth, *continue to be accountable*. Meet with a spiritual director or mature Christian who can hold you accountable to grow in Christ.

Finally, *learn to inhabit Ephesians 3:14–21* (NRSV):

> For this reason I bow my knees before the Father, from whom every family in heaven and on earth takes its name. I pray that, according to the riches of his glory, he may grant that you may be strengthened in your inner being with power through his Spirit, and that Christ may dwell in your hearts through faith, as you are being rooted and grounded in love. I pray that you may have the power to comprehend, with all the saints, what is the breadth and length and height and depth, and to know the love of Christ that surpasses knowledge, so that you may be filled with all the fullness of God.
>
> Now to him who by the power at work within us is able to accomplish abundantly far more than all we can ask or imagine, to him be glory in the church and in Christ Jesus to all generations, forever and ever. Amen.

IGNATIAN
RESOURCES

THESE IGNATIAN RESOURCES are my paraphrases based on the literal translation of the Spanish autograph by Father Elder Mullan in 1909, which was published in David Fleming's *Draw Me into Your Friendship*. In many cases, my paraphrase is very close to the literal translation.[1] My comments about the extent of paraphrase are located throughout the endnotes.

For the reader's convenience, the standard paragraph reference from Fleming's *Draw Me into Your Friendship* follows in brackets (e.g.: [313]).

Rules for Discernment

Rule 1.1 In persons who go from serious sin to serious sin, our enemy suggests to them apparent pleasures, making them imagine sensual delights in order to hold them more and make them grow in their vices and sins. The Holy Spirit uses the opposite method with these persons, pricking them and biting their consciences through the process of reason. [314]

Rule 1.2 In persons who are intensely cleansing their life and rising from good to better in the service of God our Lord, it is the method of the enemy to bite, sadden, and put obstacles, disquieting with false reasons, that one may not go on; and it is proper to the Holy Spirit to give courage and strength, consolations, tears, inspirations, and quiet, easing and removing all hindrances, that one may go on in well doing. [315]

Rule 1.3 Consolation is when we are caused to love God more. When we shed tears of love for our Lord, whether out of sorrow for our sins, or for the Passion of Christ, or because of other things directly connected with his service and praise, we are in consolation. Consolation is every increase of hope, faith and charity, and all interior joy which calls us to heavenly things, giving us peace in our Creator and Lord. [316]

Rule 1.4 Desolation is all the contrary of the first rule, such as prevailing love for things low and earthly, the unquiet of different temptations, lack of confidence in God, when we love not God, when we find ourselves all lazy, tepid, sad, and as if separated from our Creator and Lord. [317]

Rule 1.5 In times of desolation, avoid major decisions. If a decision is called for, be firm and constant in the resolutions and determination in which you were the day preceding such desolation. Because, as in consolation it is the Holy Spirit who guides and counsels us, so in desolation we are more likely to listen to bad advice from others. [318]

Rule 1.6 Although in desolation we ought not to change our first resolutions, it is very helpful to counter the desolation by insisting more on prayer, meditation, on much examination, and by giving ourselves more room to make amends. [319]

Rule 1.7 In desolation, consider how the Lord has left you in trial in your natural powers, in order to learn how to resist the different agitations and temptations of the enemy. You can resist with Divine help, which always remains with you, though you do not clearly perceive it. It only seems that the Lord has taken from you his great fervor, great love, and intense grace. [320]

Rule 1.8 In desolation, labor to be in patience, which is contrary to the vexations which come to you. Expect that you will soon be consoled, and so employ against the desolation the devices mentioned in the sixth rule. [321]

Rule 1.9 There are three principal reasons why we find ourselves desolate. The first is because we are lukewarm, lazy, or negligent in our spiritual exercises; and so through our faults, spiritual consolation withdraws from us. The second is a time of trial and shows us how much we participate in Christ's service because of our love of him, rather than love of consolation. The third is also a time of trial and it teaches us that it is not ours to get or keep great devotion, intense love, tears, or any other spiritual consolation. All consolation is a gift from God our Lord. We cannot work hard enough or be smart enough to earn a sense of God's loving presence. [322]

Rule 1.10 When you are in consolation, think of the desolation which will come after, and take new strength for then. [323]

Rule 1.11 When you are consoled, humble yourself by remembering how you are in times of desolation. On the contrary, when you are in desolation, recall that with God's grace, you can resist all your enemies by finding strength in your Creator and Lord. [324]

Rule 1.12 It is the way of our enemy to weaken and lose heart when we put on a bold front and do the opposite in the face of temptation. Yet if we begin to lose heart and have fear in the face of temptation, there is no beast as ferocious as our enemy in carrying forth his harmful intentions. [325]

Rule 1.13 Our enemy acts like a secret seducer and does not want his schemes revealed. If we confess his advances toward us to another spiritual person, he is greatly grieved because he knows that we will stand against him and not be seduced. [326]

Rule 1.14 Our enemy acts like a shrewd commander who carefully studies his enemy for weaknesses. He examines our virtues, beliefs, passions, and habits and attacks us at those places he thinks he can get a foothold. [328]

SUMMARY TEXT: PRINCIPLE AND FOUNDATION [23]

We were created to praise, reverence, and serve God our Lord, and by this means to experience salvation.[2]

All things on earth are created for us and to help us praise, reverence, and serve God. We are to use them as much as they help us in this service, and ought to rid ourselves of anything that hinders our service.

For this it is necessary that we become indifferent to all created things so that, on our part, we want not health rather than sickness, riches rather than poverty, honor rather than dishonor, long rather than short life, and so in all the rest; desiring and choosing only what helps us praise, reverence, and serve God. This detachment comes *only* if we have a stronger attachment; therefore our one dominating desire and fundamental choice must be to live in the loving presence and wisdom of Christ, our Savior.

Ignatian Parables

Kingdom Exercise[3]

Part One: In your imagination, stand before a truly good human king who says, "It is my will to rid all lands of injustice and bring them real peace. Therefore, all who would like to come with me are to be content to eat as I, and also to drink and dress, etc., as I: likewise they are to labor like me in the day and watch in the night, etc., that so afterward they may have part with me in the victory as they have had it in the labors." How should his subjects respond? [91–94]

Part Two: In your imagination, stand before Christ our King. Hear him say, "It is my will to bring all the world into the glory of my Father's kingdom; therefore, all who would like to come with me are to labor with me, that following me in the pain, they may also follow me in the glory." Consider how his subjects should respond. [95]

The Two Standards

Preparation: In your imagination, see a great battlefield. On one side sits Satan in fine array in the midst of his chief demons. The army flowing away from him are those living on the earth. They are running to do battle. They follow a flag of gold, dripping with blood. On the other side sits Jesus Christ. He is dressed simply, as are those apostles and great women standing around him. His army marches steadily and in order. They follow a flag of white, on which is embroidered a simple cross. The battle begins. [136–141]

First Point: Consider the false promises, the deceit, and the motives of the satanic command. Few people openly choose to follow Satan, and so his strategy is to seduce them by the lure of power, riches, sex, and honors. What things might your enemy tempt you with? Discuss your battle with the Lord. Ask for grace to be true to him. [142]

Second Point: Consider the humble commands of Christ. He promises suffering and trials along with joy and peace—for he will win the battle. Hear Christ call his followers to turn from worldly riches and concern for our reputations, to serve even the lowest person and to find humility as we suffer for his kingdom. Discuss your battle with Jesus. Ask for grace to be true to him. [143–146]

Third Point: See yourself on the battlefield. Through which temptations does the enemy call you to defect? Discuss your battle with Jesus. Ask for grace to be true to him.

Three Classes of People[4]

Preparation: With your imagination, consider three people. Each is typical of many others. Each one has substantial possessions. Each considers himself or herself to be moral, dutiful, and wanting to serve God. Each person is hearing Christ's call to "Follow Me." [149]

First Class: Persons in this class often say they would like to be less dependent on their possessions. They recognize that their things sometimes get in the way of serving God. They talk about the importance of serving God, but even until the end of their life they are so busy caring for what they have not given to God's service that they have made only feeble attempts to serve God. [153]

Second Class: Persons in this class would like to be free of all worldly hindrances, and be free to serve God. They develop their own plans for personal righteousness and they are quite busy about accomplishing their plans. They expect God to accept their plans and they resent giving up their possessions to keep up appearances. To the end of their days, they behave as if these things are theirs to give. [154]

Third Class: While perhaps possessing much, persons of this third class are not overly concerned with possessions. They can easily part with anything or even all that they have. As they see an advantage to God's kingdom, they quietly donate this or that or many such things. Before they purchase an item, they consider their needs, its usefulness, and its lasting value. Their time is spent performing their duties to job and family. Free time is given evenly between recreation and community (church) service. They have learned to relax and to enjoy rich relationships with other people. Other disciples admire their balance, and the way they challenge life. Their life plainly says, "God's will be done." [155]

Three Kinds of Humility[5]

First Kind: Consider the first kind of humility in which out of fear of God and his judgment, we recognize the lordship of Christ and submit the more carnal areas of our life to his rebuke and correction. [165]

Second Kind: Consider the second kind of humility in which out of love for Christ, we seek to please him in all things, large and small. This allows us a good balance in respect to work, possessions, service, family, and recreation. We seek no human recognition for their service, for we seek only God's greater glory in all areas of our life together. [166]

Third Kind: Consider the third kind of humility in which out of love for Christ and his creation, we joyfully choose poverty and persecutions in advancing his kingdom. This third kind of humility is a gift which is given to us in the proper time, and in increasing amounts, as we mature. This desire cannot be self-evoked or manipulated. Recognition of it in our life is a cause of joy—not of pride. Its absence is a call to a deeper experience of the second kind of humility. [167]

Take, Lord [234]

Take, Lord, and receive all my liberty, my memory, my intellect, and all my will—all that I have and possess. You gave them to me: to you, Lord, I return them. All is yours, dispose of all according to your will. Give me only your love and grace, for these are enough for me.

Sample Chart for Unit 2

Life Stages	Day 2 Experiences of Joy and Goodness	Day 3 Close Relationships	Day 4 My View of God	Day 5 My View of Self	Day 6 My View of Life's Purpose
8 years old, Wichita	Baking cookies with Mom	Mom, Dad, Michelle (sister), Rick	Cosmic Do-Gooder who helps me in school	Good boy	To make Mom and Dad proud
10 years old, New York City	Ice-skating in Central Park	Mom, Dad, Michelle, Samantha	Protector who keeps me safe	Studious, helpful	To make Mom and Dad proud
18 years old, Lincoln, Nebraska, College	Going to the movies with friends, my relationship with Jill	Mom, Michelle, Jill, Mike	Not sure who God is or if God exists	Cool dude, ladies' man	To have fun, make good grades
21 years old, Salt Lake City, Office Manager at Comtran Inc.	Renting my first apartment	Michelle, Doug, Karen	My friend, my Redeemer	Reluctantly accepting myself as an adult	To be a disciple and honor God
25 years old, Philadelphia, Human Resources Asst. at Apple Electric	Meeting Linda, our first dates	Michelle, Linda, Steve	God is so much wiser than I thought	I am slowly seeing I am meant to be God's man	To live with some integrity and bring glory to God

Using *Sacred*
Listening with
Groups

I HAVE HAD THE joy of leading several groups over the past two decades, which has allowed me and my coleaders to train many listeners and encourage many people to live for the greater glory of God. Because of the intense self-evaluation which is part of these Exercises, persons of some instability can make the Exercises only under a competent guide and counselor. Their presence in the group, and their input to the group, must be carefully screened. In reality, I have had very few problems. Typically, unbalanced individuals self-select out of the group within the first couple of weeks. If they can be mentored and encouraged individually, they can find some solid help within this process.

A Recommended Format for Groups

I have tried several formats, and the one laid out here is the one I have found most helpful. At the orientation meeting, I tell the story of Ignatius discovering the Exercises, introduce the basic ideas of having our lives transformed by praying Scripture, and explain the basic journaling process. This material is found in chapters 1–3. At the second meeting, I review the journaling process and describe the team-listening process. This material is found in chapter 4. After this instruction, the large group is broken into smaller listening teams of two or three and they meet for the first time to listen to the journal summaries for unit 1. There are more detailed agendas following the suggested schedules.

Forming Listening Teams

This process of forming listening teams is difficult when you do not know the people very well. I try not to make assignments. If persons in the large group have someone they want to team with, I trust they know their needs better than I do. The one exception: I generally discourage spouses from serving as listeners for each other. If assignments must be made, I try to place people with similar backgrounds in teams. I ask for disciples to be patient in this team-building process and encourage them to be flexible during the first five units. The teams have usually found each other by the end of unit 5. I try to form as many triads as possible, but if a pair of friends is committed to making the Exercises together, I allow them to remain as a pair.

Group Attendance

A successful group presentation of the Exercises requires both large group meetings and weekly team meetings. Because the process called forth by the Exercises is well under way by the second week, persons are only rarely added to the group after the second group meeting. Attendance is required as a holy obligation.

Leading the Group

The leader is responsible for the group meetings and the evaluation of group processes. He or she must be available afterward for private consultation. It is highly recommended that the leader read all of *Sacred Listening* before the orientation meeting.

Group meetings consist of four or five parts:

First, the leader takes time to review the basic instructions and to check for any problems with the listening process. This takes longer in the beginning weeks, usually about thirty minutes. Once people relax, this step takes only a few minutes.

Second, the leader allows an hour for listening teams to listen to and discuss the weekly journal summaries.

Third, the leader presents a *lectio divina* to the entire group as follows: After selecting an appropriate text from the units before or as suggested in the agendas below, read the text out loud and then wait in silence for 3–4 minutes. Repeat this twice, and then invite disciples to respond with single sentences of confession, praise, and thanksgiving. Close this time by saying the Lord's Prayer together. Time permitting, I follow this with a brief period of teaching addressing the content of the *lectio*.

Fourth, if a Rule for Discernment has been introduced in the previous week(s), I ask for people to share their experiences of the rule.

Finally, I provide some orientation for the coming week(s).

I limit these meetings to two hours. With larger groups, I plan to stay an hour or two to work with individuals who still have questions.

Suggested Schedule and Agenda

The following schedule is for group meetings held on Saturdays from September through May. Suggested start date for Meeting 1 (Orientation) is week 39 of the calendar year. Meeting 6 normally falls on the second Saturday of December, with time allowed for Thanksgiving break between meetings 4 and 5.

Meeting 7 starts the first or second week of January, and the subsequent meeting dates are scheduled so that Meeting 12 falls on the Saturday after Easter. (Note that unit 21 is scheduled for disciples to begin on Easter Sunday.) Schedule three weeks between Meeting 11, which includes the Decision-Making Unit, and Meeting 12.

Included in the chart below are several sample years to help you with your scheduling.

Meeting #	2006–2007	2007–2008	2008–2009	Topic/ Unit
1	9/30	9/29	9/27	Orientation to *Sacred Listening*, and testimonies from past participants
				ASSIGNMENT: Unit 1; Read *Sacred Listening*, chapters 2–4
2	10/7	10/6	10/4	Introduction to the Listening Team process, first Listening Team meeting
				ASSIGNMENT: Units 2 & 3

Meeting #	2006– 2007	2007– 2008	2008– 2009	Topic/ Unit
3	10/28	10/27	10/25	Understanding the Principle and Foundation
				ASSIGNMENT: Units 4 & 5
4	11/18	11/17	11/15	Understanding the Rules for Discernment
				ASSIGNMENT: Units 6 & 7 (Try to take some time off for Thanksgiving)
5	12/9	12/8	12/6	Understanding our sin histories and the fifth Rule for Discernment
				ASSIGNMENT: Unit 8
6	12/16	12/15	12/13	Summary and preparing for the incarnation and ministry of Jesus
				ASSIGNMENT: Units 9 (with optional 9A) & 10
7	1/6	1/5	1/10	Using the Ignatian parables
				ASSIGNMENT: Units 11 & 12
8	1/20	1/19	1/24	Grappling with the Two Standards
				ASSIGNMENT: Units 13 & 14
9	2/3	2/2	2/7	Understanding Three Kinds of People
				ASSIGNMENT: Units 15 & 16
10	2/24	2/16	2/28	Recognizing the Three Kinds of Humility in our daily lives
				ASSIGNMENT: Units 17 & 18, Decision-Making Unit (optional)
11*	3/17 4/8	3/8 3/23	3/21 4/12	Summary and preparation for the crucifixion
				ASSIGNMENT: Units 19–21
				*Easter: Begin unit 21 on Easter Sunday
12	4/14	3/29	4/18	Living with a resurrected Lord
				ASSIGNMENT: Units 22 & 23
13	4/28	4/19	5/9	Understanding our lives as pilgrimage
				ASSIGNMENT: Unit 24
14	5/5	4/26	5/16	Celebration!

Agenda

As previously mentioned, the leader should be familiar with *Sacred Listening* by the first meeting. You may encourage all participants to read chapter 1 before the orientation.

Below is a sample group meeting agenda that coincides with the schedule above.

Meeting 1 Orientation to *Sacred Listening*, testimonies from past participants

ASSIGNMENT: Unit 1; Read chaps. 2, 3 & 4 in *Sacred Listening*
1. Prayer. Welcome and brief personal introductions. In groups of five, discuss any prior experience with the *Spiritual Exercises* and other discipleship programs.
2. Instructions for using our imaginations as we pray with Scripture (Using Your Imagination, pp. 23–24).
3. *Lectio divina:* Luke 7:36–50. Hear this text as the woman, respond after the third reading with a single-sentence observation or thanksgiving (Reading Scripture, pp. 22–23).

(Break)
4. The life of Ignatius as a model (What Are the Spiritual Exercises? pp. 13–16).
5. Journaling (chap. 3, pp. 34–43), with special emphasis on guidelines for reviewing your journal (p. 43).
6. Prayer for encouragement.

Meeting 2 Introduction to the Listening Team process, first Listening Team meeting

ASSIGNMENT: Units 2 & 3
1. Prayer. In small groups, discuss "How is the journaling process working for you?" Prepare one question or observation for a larger group discussion.
2. Questions and observations on the journaling process.
3. Review guidelines for listening to journal summaries (pp. 51–52) and listen to each other in teams of three.
   Reminder for Third Listeners: Your key purpose is to pray and listen to God in the midst of the conversation between the disciple and her/his listener. You don't need to say anything.

(Break)
4. Regroup for questions.
5. *Lectio divina:* 2 Corinthians 4.

6. Brief orientation to units 2 and 3. Prayer for encouragement.

Meeting 3 Understanding the Principle and Foundation

ASSIGNMENT: Units 4 & 5

1. Prayer. In small groups, discuss "How is the process of listening to one another working for you?" Prepare one question or observation for a larger group discussion.
2. Questions and observations on the listening process.
3. Listen to each other in teams of two or three. Repeat "Reminder for Third Listeners."

(Break)

4. *Lectio divina:* John 4:1–19.
5. Brief orientation to units 4 and 5, understanding the Principle and Foundation.
6. Prayer for encouragement.

Meeting 4 Understanding the Rules for Discernment

ASSIGNMENT: Units 6 & 7

1. Prayer. In small groups that do not include your normal listening partner, discuss "How is the process of listening to one another working for you?" Prepare one question or observation for a larger group discussion.
2. Questions and observations on the listening process.
3. Listen to each other in teams of two or three. Repeat "Reminder for Third Listeners."

(Break)

4. *Lectio divina:* Luke 18:18–30.
5. Brief orientation to units 6 and 7, understanding the Rules for Discernment.
6. Prayer for encouragement.

Meeting 5 Understanding our sin histories and the fifth Rule for Discernment

ASSIGNMENT: Unit 8

1. Prayer. In small groups that do not include your normal listening partner, discuss "How is the process of listening to one another working for you?" Prepare one question or observation for a larger group discussion.
2. Questions and observations on the listening process.

3. Listen to each other in teams of two or three. Remember to pray *for* one another. Repeat "Reminder for Third Listeners."

(Break)

4. *Lectio divina:* Philippians 3:1–17.
5. Understanding our sin histories and the fifth Rule for Discernment.
6. Brief orientation to unit 8. Comments about "godly sorrow" and "worldly sorrow" from 2 Corinthians 7:10–11.
7. Prayer for encouragement.

Meeting 6 Summary and preparing for the incarnation and ministry of Jesus

ASSIGNMENT: Units 9 (and optional Unit 9A) & 10

1. Prayer. In small groups that do not include your normal listening partner, discuss "How is the process of listening to one another working for you?" Prepare one question or observation for a larger group discussion.
2. Questions and observations on the listening process.
3. Listen to each other in teams of two or three. Remember to pray *for* one another. Repeat "Reminder for Third Listeners."

(Break)

4. *Lectio divina:* Psalm 37:1–16.
5. Share experiences of the fifth Rule for Discernment.
6. Brief orientation to units 9 and 10; review Using Your Imagination (pp. 23–24).
7. Prayer for encouragement.

Meeting 7 Using the Ignatian parables

ASSIGNMENT: Units 11 & 12

1. Prayer. In small groups that do not include your normal listening partner, discuss "How is the process of listening to one another working for you?" Prepare one question or observation for a larger group discussion.
2. Questions and observations on the listening process.
3. Listen to each other in teams of two or three. Remember to pray *for* one another. Repeat "Reminder for Third Listeners."

(Break)

4. *Lectio divina:* Colossians 1:9–14.
5. Share experiences of the seventh and eighth Rules for Discernment.
6. Using Ignatian parables and a brief orientation to units 11 and 12.
7. Prayer for encouragement.

Meeting 8 Grappling with the Two Standards

ASSIGNMENT: Units 13 & 14

1. Prayer. In small groups that do not include your normal listening partner, discuss "How are you experiencing the Kingdom Exercise in daily life?" Prepare one question or observation for a larger group discussion.
2. Questions and observations on the Kingdom Exercise.
3. Listen to each other in teams of two or three. Remember to pray *for* one another. Repeat "Reminder for Third Listeners."

(Break)

4. *Lectio divina:* Psalm 49.
5. Share experiences of the ninth Rule for Discernment.
6. Using Ignatian parables and a brief orientation to units 13 and 14.
7. Prayer for encouragement.

Meeting 9 Understanding Three Kinds of People

ASSIGNMENT: Units 15 & 16

1. Prayer. In small groups that do not include your normal listening partner, discuss "How are the Ignatian parables working for you?" Prepare one question or observation for a larger group discussion.
2. Questions and observations on the listening process and experiences of the Ignatian parables.
3. Listen to each other in teams of two or three. Remember to pray *for* one another. Repeat "Reminder for Third Listeners."

(Break)

4. *Lectio divina:* Mark 12:38–44.
5. Share experiences of the fifth and ninth Rules for Discernment.
6. Using Ignatian parables and a brief orientation to units 15 and 16.
7. Prayer for encouragement.

Meeting 10 Recognizing the Three Kinds of Humility in our daily lives

ASSIGNMENT: Units 17 & 18

1. Prayer. In small groups that do not include your normal listening partner, discuss "How are the Ignatian parables working for you?" Prepare one question or observation for a larger group discussion.
2. Questions and observations on the listening process and experiences of the Ignatian parables.
3. Listen to each other in teams of two or three. Remember to pray *for* one another. Repeat "Reminder for Third Listeners."

(Break)

4. *Lectio divina:* Philippians 3:3–14.
5. Understanding the Three Kinds of Humility.
6. A brief orientation to units 17 and 18.
7. Using the Ignatian Decision-Making Unit.
8. Prayer for encouragement.

Meeting 11 Summary and preparation for the crucifixion

ASSIGNMENT: Units 19–21; Begin Unit 21 on Easter Sunday
1. Prayer. In small groups that do not include your normal listening partner, discuss "How am I experiencing the Principle and Foundation?"
   Prepare one question or observation for a larger group discussion.
2. Questions and observations with the larger group.
3. Listen to each other in teams of two or three. Remember to pray
   for one another. Repeat "Reminder for Third Listeners."
(Break)
4. *Lectio divina:* Colossians 1:24–29.
5. Understanding our participation in the suffering of Jesus.
6. A brief orientation to units 19–20.
7. Prayer for encouragement.
8. Remind group to begin unit 21 on Easter Sunday.

Meeting 12 Living with a resurrected Lord

ASSIGNMENT: Units 22 & 23
1. Prayer. In small groups that do not include your normal listening
   partner, discuss "How is my experience of the resurrection deepened
   by my experience of the cross?" Prepare one question or observation
   for a larger group discussion.
2. Questions and observations with the larger group.
3. Listen to each other in teams of two or three. Remember to pray
   for one another. Repeat "Reminder for Third Listeners."
(Break)
4. *Lectio divina:* Colossians 2:6–19.
5. Understanding our participation in the resurrection of Jesus.
6. A brief orientation to units 22–23.
7. Prayer for encouragement.

Meeting 13 Understanding our lives as pilgrimage

ASSIGNMENT: Unit 24
1. Prayer. In small groups that do not include your normal listening
   partner, discuss "How is my experience of the resurrection deepened

by my experience of the cross?" Prepare one question or observation for a larger group discussion.

2. Questions and observations with the larger group.
3. Listen to each other in teams of two or three. Remember to pray *for* one another. Repeat "Reminder for Third Listeners."

(Break)

4. *Lectio divina:* Colossians 3:1–11.
5. Understanding our participation in the resurrection of Jesus.
6. Emphasize the instructions for the expanded *contemplatio* as given in unit 24.
7. Prayer for encouragement.

Meeting 14 Celebration!
1. Time for success stories.
2. *Lectio divina:* Colossians 3:12–17.
3. Communion.

NOTES

Preface

1. "What Is Your World Like? A Reader's Guide to a Christian World View," *Discipleship Journal* 23 (1984), 36.

2. John A. Veltri, S.J., *Orientations*, vol. 2 (Guelph, ON: Loyola House, 1981). David L. Fleming, S.J., *The Spiritual Exercises of St. Ignatius: A Literal Translation and Contemporary Reading* (St. Louis: Institute of Jesuit Sources, 1978), revised as *Draw Me into Your Friendship: A Literal Translation and a Contemporary Reading of The Spiritual Exercises* (St. Louis: Institute of Jesuit Sources, 1996).

3. Those familiar with the *Spiritual Exercises* in their more traditional forms will notice my changes focus on how we should use the Rules for Discernment. I have found that it is intensely valuable for disciples to learn and pray with the first set of Rules for Discernment.

4. Salt Lake Theological Seminary was founded as the Utah Institute for Biblical Studies in 1984. This institute evolved into a seminary and changed its name when it began offering graduate courses in 1998.

5. Fr. Armand Nigro, S.J., director of the Mater Dei Institute at Gonzaga University, was kind enough to read the first self-published edition. He offered many helpful suggestions in April 1987. I received generous comments from John Sheets, S.J., and Thomas Green, S.J., in 1990. I completed my doctoral studies at a good Jesuit university (Marquette) in 2001. I continue to be amazed at the generosity and kindness of that entire faculty.

Chapter 1 An Introduction to the Spiritual Exercises

1. This brief account is drawn from *A Pilgrim's Journey: The Autobiography of Ignatius of Loyola*, trans. Joseph N. Tylenda, S.J. (Wilmington, DE: Michael Glazier, 1985), xiv–xix, 7–44. For the sake of readers who are using other editions, below I will include the standard paragraph references of this biography in brackets, e.g., [1–37].

2. See John W. O'Malley, S.J., *The First Jesuits* (Cambridge, MA: Harvard, 1993), 24.

3. *A Pilgrim's Journey*, 15 [8].

4. Ibid., 22 [14].

5. The meditations came from García Jiménez de Cisneros, *Exercitatory of the Spiritual Life*, circa 1500. He was the

former abbot, and his manual was still in use in the abbey. Joseph N. Tylenda, S.J., records these details in the notes to paragraph 17 in *A Pilgrim's Journey*, 25. And see O'Malley, *The First Jesuits*, 24.

6. O'Malley credits Ludolph's volume as the most important source behind the Exercises, and as having had "an extensive impact on the structure of the *Exercises*, on the style and content of the method of prayer." See *The First Jesuits*, 46.

7. See ibid., 35.

8. Again, because of space constraints, I cannot give even the briefest introduction to the early history of the Jesuits. Those wanting a precise introduction should begin with O'Malley, *The First Jesuits*.

9. Good summaries of the *Spiritual Exercises* from a Jesuit perspective can be found in David L. Fleming, S.J., *Notes on the Spiritual Exercises of St. Ignatius of Loyola* (St. Louis: Review for Religious, 1983), 2–18; and in O'Malley, *The First Jesuits*, 37–50. Ignatius's own summary is found in his "Fourth Annotation" or preliminary note on giving the Exercises. See Fleming, *Draw Me into Your Friendship*, 6.

10. The Jesuits have debated at some length as to whether the *Spiritual Exercises* should be used exclusively for making vocational choices, or as to whether they might also be used as a school of prayer (see O'Malley, *The First Jesuits*, 38–40, 47, 128–31). Definitive evidence of their common use as a school of prayer may be drawn from the Official Directory of 1599. See Martin E. Palmer, S.J., trans. and ed., *On Giving the Spiritual Exercises: The Early Jesuit Manuscript Directories and the Official Directory of 1599* (St. Louis: Institute of Jesuit Sources, 1996), 307. In what follows, I have tried to capitalize on the *Spiritual Exercises* as a school of prayer and so deal very little with vocational choices. My reasons are simple: the discernment of vocation is both too important and too

complex to attempt without an accessible and experienced mentor.

11. An excellent program for an eight- or twelve-day retreat is presented in Thomas H. Green, S.J., *A Vacation with the Lord* (Notre Dame, IN: Ave Maria Press, 1986), rev. ed. (San Francisco: Ignatius Press, 2000). Also, see John J. English, S.J., *Spiritual Freedom: From an Experience of the Ignatian Exercises to the Art of Spiritual Guidance*, 2nd ed. (Chicago: Loyola Press, 1995), 54, for brief counsel on what is appropriate in an eight-day retreat.

12. An hour and a half is best, with an hour for prayer and thirty minutes for a review of life. I give more detailed instructions for this in chapter 2, Making These Exercises. However, many people have made good progress with only an hour, and so I suggest an hour as an expected minimum. See Fleming, *Draw Me into Your Friendship*, 19.

13. See O'Malley, *The First Jesuits*, 39, and please see my testimony of ongoing conversion in the *Sacred Listening* preface.

14. As an aid to spiritual directors using other versions, I include the standard paragraph references within brackets, e.g., [para. 4].

15. One advantage of avoiding the term *week* here is that often disciples need more than seven consecutive days to complete the meditations.

16. Although the "Rules of the First Week for Discerning Spirits" are seldom given to disciples in more traditional programs, I have found great benefit in giving them as the subject of meditation. Several dynamics are encouraged by this. I mention two benefits here: First, the disciples are more directly responsible for discernment and so are more independent of the guide. See English, *Spiritual Freedom*, 122, for an exhortation to teach disciples "to handle their own problems." Second, and most important, the rules help train

the disciples' attention, and so makes these Exercises an intensely practical laboratory for lifelong spiritual awareness. Ignatius anticipated this in part in his eighth annotation. Fleming suggests directors may choose to give the rules to disciples in his paraphrase of the tenth annotation, as does English (*Spiritual Freedom*, 123). On the other hand, the ninth annotation cautions us against giving the "Rules for the Second Week" to those not being tempted under the appearance of good. See Fleming, *Draw Me into Your Friendship*, 11 [para. 8–10].

17. In this regard, pastors, group leaders, and directors will want to study discussions of Ignatius's eighteenth annotation. Ignatius is somewhat vague on this point. Briefly, he suggests some may not have sufficient talent or ability, some personality types may not fit well, and some persons are simply not called of God to make the rest of the *Spiritual Exercises*. See also Palmer, *On Giving the Spiritual Exercises*, 294.

18. Thomas H. Green puts the difference between the first and second movements (weeks) nicely: "The retreatant has come to an honest, Spirit-guided knowledge of himself or herself—to a vision of self as seen by God—in the first week. In the second week, he or she has turned from self knowledge to a contemplation of Jesus Christ in his public life on earth. Having come 'naked' before the Lord in the first week, the retreatant now seeks to put on the Lord Jesus Christ, to be filled with Christ." See Thomas H. Green, *Weeds among the Wheat* (Notre Dame, IN: Ave Maria Press, 1984), 60.

19. In this manual, I encourage disciples offended by his military imagery to rephrase his parables so that they are more appropriate to their own contexts.

20. An optional unit that teaches one of the Ignatian methods for making decisions follows unit 18.

21. The necessity of giving assignments in writing was recognized already in the Official Directory of 1599. See Martin E. Palmer, S.J., trans. and ed., *On Giving the Spiritual Exercises: The Early Jesuit Manuscript Directories and the Official Directory of 1599* (St. Louis: Institute of Jesuit Sources, 1996), 307. One can imagine this taking very different forms. The similarity in form to John A. Veltri, S.J., *Orientations, Volume II: A Manual to Aid Beginning Spiritual Directors of the Spiritual Exercises according to Annotation 19* (Guelph, ON: Loyola House, 1981) is not accidental. My spiritual director made a forty-day retreat in Guelph, September 28–November 7, 1983. Under the supervision of John Sheets, S.J., she used Father Veltri's manual to form our assignments, and so I prayed and lived with this form for thirty weeks in 1984–1985. I adapted Father Veltri's form initially for use with Baptists in 1985, and then again with Lutherans in 1986. In the course of two decades, I have changed many things from those early versions, but the form has held true. And now I am delighted to discover he revised his small volume from 1981 into more than six hundred pages of helps "for those who accompany others on the inward journey." See John A. Veltri, S.J., *Orientations, Volume II: Part A* (Guelph, ON: Guelph Centre of Spirituality, 1998), and *Orientations, Volume II: Part B* (Guelph, ON: Guelph Centre of Spirituality, 1998). He presents a plan for a thirty-week retreat in part A, pp. 197–260. Those who find a calling as spiritual directors will want to study his work closely. My own debt to him remains profound.

Chapter 2 Making These Exercises

1. See English, *Spiritual Freedom*, 18; the sixteenth annotation in Fleming's *Draw Me into Your Friendship*, 14 [para.

16]; and Fleming's own paraphrase of the purpose of the *Spiritual Exercises* in *Draw Me into Your Friendship*, 23 [para. 21].

2. Ignatius wanted this discussion to be as deep and searching as possible, and so he often assigned what is called the "Triple Colloquy," in which disciples discussed the subject at hand with Mary, with Jesus, and then with our Father. Fewer Protestants would be comfortable with this, and so I ask disciples to "discuss your meditation with your Lord." Ignatius himself suggested this in a note to the Third Week. See Fleming, *Draw Me into Your Friendship*, 54–57 [para. 63], and 150 [para. 199].

3. To learn more about the practice of the "divine reading," see Eugene H. Peterson's lively discussion of the *lectio divina* in *Eat This Book: A Conversation in the Art of Spiritual Reading* (Grand Rapids: Eerdmans, 2006), 90–117. The quotation is from page 116, with the italic emphasis in the original. See also Gordon T. Smith, *The Voice of Jesus: Discernment, Prayer, and the Witness of the Spirit* (Downers Grove, IL: InterVarsity, 2003), 121–26.

4. Sadly, a popular book in the mid-1980s labeled almost all use of the imagination as idolatrous. See Dave Hunt and T.A. McMahon, *The Seduction of Christianity: Spiritual Discernment in the Last Days* (Eugene, OR: Harvest House, 1985), 161–69. A more substantial reservation rises within Reformed theology from John Calvin's theology of revelation. For this, see Peter Adams, *Hearing God's Words: Exploring Biblical Spirituality*, New Studies in Biblical Theology 16 (Downers Grove, IL: InterVarsity, 2004). His fourth chapter details Calvin's theology of revelation, and his fifth chapter includes a helpful discussion of the use of images on pages 146–47 and 173. But that this analysis does not preclude what we are suggesting here is evidenced by his discussion of Richard Baxter on meditation on pages 202–10. His inclusion of Baxter's advice to use our senses in meditation and prayer on pages 208–9 comes close to the Ignatian methods described in *Sacred Listening*.

5. Italics added. This sixth note from the "Notes on the Translation of the Greek Tenses" appears just after the Editorial Board's preface in the *New American Standard Bible: New Testament* (Cleveland and New York: World Publishing Company, 1960). Later editions included a similar note as the last of their "Explanation of General Format." See *New American Standard Bible* (Nashville: Thomas Nelson, 1977).

6. Not everyone has been afraid to use his or her imagination. Eugene Peterson gives an impassioned and eloquent plea to read Scripture with our imagination and all five senses in *Reversed Thunder: The Revelation of John and the Praying Imagination* (San Francisco: Harper & Row, 1988), 14–17. Warren W. Wiersbe offers us much good counsel in *Preaching and Teaching with Imagination: The Quest for Biblical Ministry* (Grand Rapids: Baker, 1994). Special note should be made of Gregory A. Boyd, *Seeing Is Believing: Experiencing Jesus through Imaginative Prayer* (Grand Rapids: Baker, 2004). Note especially his gentle answer to J. I. Packer's worries about idolatry in the use of mental imagery on pages 135–39.

7. It is unfortunate that many clergy have no experience with the Exercises. If this is the case, clergy might consider doing the Exercises with two mature laypersons. This investment of time will be returned many times in the future. A second choice would be to contact Tom Ashbrook, director of spiritual formation with Church Resource Ministries. He is willing to help connect clergy with experienced listeners if none can be found in their immediate region.

8. Tom Ashbrook reports: "I have coached/listened to dozens of folks over email. They send me their journal by unit, and I respond briefly to each journal entry. This then is supplemented by occasional phone calls."

9. These Exercises are highly structured. Historically, the *Spiritual Exercises* are given to a disciple in small blocks of instruction and discussed daily or weekly. Adjustments are made by a well-trained spiritual director as needed at each point, so that the *Spiritual Exercises* are highly individualized. This is undoubtedly the surest way to growth. But there are few directors skilled enough to direct the great number of people who are seeking a deeper relationship with Christ. *Sacred Listening* attempts to minimize the need for a trained spiritual director. This call for flexibility is meant to keep the assignments from becoming a straitjacket.

10. James I. Packer, *Keep in Step with the Spirit* (Old Tappan, NJ: Revell, 1984), 106.

11. Gerard Hughes, *God of Surprises* (New York: Paulist Press, 1985), 27–29, points out the paradox in this text.

12. See Gordon T. Smith's helpful discussion of this in *The Voice of Jesus*, 89–108, and especially 102.

13. Ignatius's thirteenth Rule for Discernment tells us that Satan is greatly "dispirited" when we inform a spiritually mature person of the temptations we are facing.

14. The alert reader will note this is the functional definition of *grace* used throughout the *Spiritual Exercises*. See English, *Spiritual Freedom*, 61, 94, and 141.

15. See Jules J. Toner, S.J., *A Commentary on Saint Ignatius' Rules for the Discernment of Spirits* (St. Louis: Institute of Jesuit Sources, 1982), 9.

Chapter 3 How to Keep a Spiritual Journal

1. See Gary R. Collins, *The Magnificent Mind* (Waco: Word, 1985), 107–17 for an accessible description of this complicated process.

2. Thomas H. Green, S.J., *A Vacation with the Lord* (San Francisco: Ignatius Press, 2000), 21–23, and *Weeds among the Wheat*, 148–49.

3. Gordon MacDonald, *Ordering Your Private World* (Nashville: Thomas Nelson, 1985), 131–32, italics added. MacDonald has continued to write about the benefits of keeping a journal, and so see also his "Journaling: A Tool to Bring Your Soul into Focus," *Leadership Journal* 25, no. 3 (2004): 88ff.

4. See Dallas Willard, *In Search of Guidance* (Ventura, CA: Regal, 1984), 229. This was reprinted as *Hearing God: Developing a Conversational Relationship with God* (Downers Grove, IL: InterVarsity, 1999), 199–200.

5. This is intended as a soft version of what is known as the daily examen. See Fleming, *Draw Me into Your Friendship*, 33 [para. 32–43]. In light of the counsel given in the Official Directory of 1599, *Sacred Listening* provides a stronger version of the daily examen in preparation for completing the Exercises in unit 24. See Palmer, *On Giving the Spiritual Exercises*, 313. For crisp advice on why the review must take place after we pray, see English, *Spiritual Freedom*, 53.

6. See Fleming, *Draw Me into Your Friendship*, 68–69 [para. 77].

7. Smith, *The Voice of Jesus*, 39.

8. See O'Malley, *The First Jesuits*, 41–42.

9. The Official Directory of 1599 counsels that our time for reading and writing should be moderate so that we can give ourselves to our meditation and prayer.

See Palmer, *On Giving the Spiritual Exercises*, 297.

10. Tom Ashbrook shared these insights with me in an email dated April 7, 2005.

Chapter 4 Instructions for Listeners

1. One could multiply authorities making this point. I suggest one in particular for persons new to the practices of spiritual direction. See Jeannette A. Bakke, *Holy Invitations: Exploring Spiritual Direction* (Grand Rapids: Baker, 2000), 31, 122, 137, 157.

2. See 2 Timothy 3:16–17 and Ephesians 4:11–16.

3. Romans 8:26–27.

4. Thomas A. Hart, *The Art of Christian Listening* (Ramsey, NJ: Paulist Press, 1980), 17. I highly recommend Hart's book to each person who listens. It is profitable reading and has stood the test of many years.

5. Listeners will be comforted by meditating on Jeremiah 31:33–34.

6. See John 16:13–16.

7. See Tilden H. Edwards, *Spiritual Friend* (New York: Paulist Press, 1980), 162.

8. William A. Barry, S.J., "On Asking God to Reveal Himself in Retreat," in *Notes on the Spiritual Exercises of St. Ignatius of Loyola*, ed. David L. Fleming, S.J. (St. Louis: Review for Religious, 1983), 74.

9. William A. Barry, S.J., and William J. Connolly, S.J., *The Practice of Spiritual Direction* (Minneapolis: Seabury Press, 1982), 93.

10. Ibid., 98. And consider these wise comments from English, *Spiritual Freedom*: "The retreatant belongs to Jesus, not the guide. Many of the difficulties the guide struggles with can be handled much better by the Holy Spirit" (46); and "Normally, even though guides think they

recognize the pattern of a retreatant's life, it is better to let the retreatant find it out for himself or herself. It is far better for the Spirit to lead the individual to deeper self-understanding. The Spirit will certainly do so when the person is ready" (158).

11. For a helpful discussion of some of the differences between counseling and spiritual direction, see Gerald May, *Care of Mind, Care of Spirit* (San Francisco: Harper & Row, 1982), 12–17.

12. Fleming, *Draw Me into Your Friendship*, 14 [para. 15]. Fleming's paraphrase puts it plainly: "God is not only our Creator but also the Director of our retreat, and the human director should never provide a hindrance to such an intimate communication" (15).

13. Francis Kelly Nemeck and Marie Theresa Coombs, *The Way of Spiritual Direction* (Wilmington, DE: Michael Glazier, 1985), 189.

14. They can be contacted at www.shalem.org. The books by Hart, Conroy, and Bakke listed in the bibliography are especially recommended as you begin listening.

15. The need for good spiritual directors or listeners is humorously portrayed in Eugene Peterson's "The Summer of My Discontent," *Christianity Today*, January 15, 1990, 28–30.

The First Movement

1. John J. English, S.J., wisely counsels that at the outset of the Exercises, retreatants should have three days of "prayer on God's love for humanity." I take this advice to heart, and so focus the first four units in deepening our experience of God's love for us in good times, times of trial, and times of rebellion. This first week surveys many of the gifts we will seek from God. See *Spiritual Freedom: From an Experience of the Ignatian Exercises to the Art of Spiri-*

tual Guidance, 2nd ed. (Chicago: Loyola Press, 1995), 41.

2. From Ludolph of Saxony, *Life of Christ*, as quoted in Gerard W. Hughes, *God of Surprises* (New York: Paulist Press, 1985), 53. Although Ignatius instructs us to use all five senses somewhat later in the Exercises, our experience with many disciples shows it is helpful for many people even in these earlier meditations. See David L. Fleming, S.J., *Draw Me into Your Friendship: A Literal Translation and a Contemporary Reading of The Spiritual Exercises* (St. Louis: Institute of Jesuit Sources, 1996), 58 [para. 65–70]. If your conscience is sensitive about this use of your imagination in prayer, please review Using Your Imagination in chapter 2. And remember, we are not trying to change or influence the events.

3. See Fleming, *Draw Me into Your Friendship*, 246–49 [para. 314–15]. Strictly speaking, these are Rules for the First Week.

4. Units 2 and 3 are designed to help disciples notice the consolation they have received from God's presence in their happier times. Both are intended to help prepare disciples for the more difficult review of times of rebellion in unit 4 and to give them courage to make a good confession at the end of unit 8. Experienced directors will recognize this as providing an intuitive experience of Rule 1.3, and invokes the logic of Rules 1.10 and 1.11 as disciples are prepared for possible experiences of desolation.

5. The idea of using charts is not part of the original *Spiritual Exercises*. I developed them to help more visual learners bring their meditations into focus. They are patterned after the charts in James W. Fowler, *Faith Development and Pastoral Care* (Philadelphia: Fortress Press, 1987), 124–25.

6. This grace is, of course, related to the first point of the daily examen. See

Fleming, *Draw Me into Your Friendship*, 38 [para. 43].

7. These helps to our memory are adapted from Ignatius's suggestion that we consider our place and house, our relations, and our occupation as aids to remembering our sin histories. See Fleming, *Draw Me into Your Friendship*, 50 [para. 56].

8. See Fleming, *Draw Me into Your Friendship*, 220 [para. 279].

9. This grace is suggested, in part, in response to helpful observations on our experience of sin and salvation in English, *Spiritual Freedom*, 63.

10. The literal translation assigns disciples to ask for "shame and confusion at myself, seeing how many have been damned for only one mortal sin, and how many times I deserve to be condemned forever for my so many sins." See Fleming, *Draw Me into Your Friendship*, 42 [para. 48].

11. Although Ignatius does not assign such an imaginative role play until the second week, we have found it useful to introduce this in coming to understand God's love for us. See Fleming, *Draw Me into Your Friendship*, 96 [para. 114].

12. See ibid., 44 [para. 50].

13. See ibid., 46 [para. 51].

14. See ibid., 248–250 [para. 316–17].

15. See ibid., 50 [para. 55]. Here I am close to Ignatius, and yet I attempt to balance the grace he suggests with the intent of the entire first movement.

16. This is a slight rephrasing of Ignatius's own words. See ibid., 52 [para. 52].

17. See ibid., 222 [para. 282].

18. Here I depart significantly from the suggested grace: "Ask for the interior sense of pain which the damned suffer, in order that, if through my faults, I should forget the love of the Eternal Lord, at least the fear of the pains may help me not to come into sin." See Fleming, *Draw Me into Your Friendship*, 58 [para. 65].

19. See ibid., 252 [para. 318].

20. See ibid., 252 [para. 319].

21. See ibid., 58 [para. 65–70].

22. See Palmer, *On Giving the Spiritual Exercise*, 317–18; and see Fleming, *Draw Me into Your Friendship*, 41 [para. 44]. One comment by John English needs to be understood carefully in this. He observes: "The Exercises are not meant as an examination of a person's sinful life in order to prepare for the sacrament of reconciliation" (see English, *Spiritual Freedom*, 48). We can agree this is not the intended purpose of the Exercises. And we can admit that if such confession helps disciples accept God's love, this is an appropriate time to confess our sins one to another, as counseled in James 5:16.

The Second Movement

1. Here I am attempting to honor the wisdom of William A. Barry, S.J., as he reminds us this is Ignatius's *affective* Principle and Foundation. See *Letting God Come Close: An Approach to the Ignatian Spiritual Exercises* (Chicago: Loyola Press, 2001), 6, 70–77.

2. Ignatius recognized this possibility with these phrases: "if the person who is making the Exercises is old or weak, or, although strong, has become in some way less strong from the first week . . ." See Fleming, *Draw Me into Your Friendship*, 102 [para. 129].

3. See English, *Spiritual Freedom*, 131–34, for a description of this movement from meditation to contemplation.

4. See ibid., 206 [para. 262].

5. See ibid., 208 [para. 263].

6. See ibid., 208 [para. 264].

7. See ibid., 96 [para. 114].

8. See ibid., 208 [para. 264–65].

9. I am highlighting the theme of poverty with the shepherds as opposed to suggesting it in a less-embodied experience. See ibid., 98 [para. 116].

10. This is an attempt to help disciples take the more cosmic perspective encouraged in the third point of the first contemplation. See ibid., 94 [para. 108].

11. See ibid., 210 [para. 266].

12. See ibid., 210 [para. 268].

13. See ibid., 210 [para. 267].

14. Again, I am highlighting the theme of poverty with the wise men as opposed to suggesting it in a less-embodied experience. See ibid., 98 [para. 116].

15. See ibid., 212 [para. 269].

16. See ibid., 212 [para. 272].

17. From Ludolph of Saxony, *Life of Christ*, as quoted in Gerard W. Hughes, *God of Surprises* (New York: Paulist Press, 1985), 53.

18. See Fleming, *Draw Me into Your Friendship*, 212 [para. 271]. I am adding the text from Hebrews to help people feel permission to use their imaginations more freely here.

19. See ibid., 214 [para. 273].

20. See ibid., 214 [para. 274].

21. See ibid., 252 [para. 320–21].

22. I am agreeing here with John J. English, S.J., that the purpose of the Kingdom Exercise is "merely to instill generosity and openness to God's will" (see *Spiritual Freedom*, 104).

23. This is my paraphrase of the second prelude to the "Call of the Temporal King." See Fleming, *Draw Me into Your Friendship*, 82 [para. 91].

24. John English, S.J., wisely counsels that this exercise is not meant to lead to another examination of our conscience. Rather, it aims to help us "understand the deceits of the evil one." See English, *Spiritual Freedom*, 147.

25. This grace is a rephrasing of the Third Prelude: "ask for knowledge of the deceits of the bad chief and help to guard myself against them, and for knowledge of the true life which the supreme and good captain shows and grace to imitate him."

See Fleming, *Draw Me into Your Friendship*, 110 [para. 139].

26. See ibid., 110–14 [para. 136–48]. I am minimizing the graphic imagery of the demonic [para. 140–42]. I make less of the call to poverty [para. 146] in light of the coming meditations on the Three Classes of People and Three Kinds of Humility.

27. See ibid., 222 [para. 283]. Ignatius assigned Matthew 14:13–21 for the feeding of the five thousand.

28. The third reason is substantially rephrased. See ibid., 254 [para. 322].

29. See ibid., 216 [para. 275].

30. Again, this is with minimal rephrasing. See ibid., 254 [para. 323–24].

31. This is a rephrasing of the Third Prelude. See ibid., 116 [para. 152].

32. For more on this, see the careful comments in English, *Spiritual Freedom*, 164–65. His comments on page 164 have helped me shape the grace as well.

33. I have significantly rephrased this to avoid some unhappy stereotypes of both men and women. See Fleming, *Draw Me into Your Friendship*, 256 [para. 325].

34. I have significantly rephrased this to avoid unnecessary color and verbiage. See ibid., 256 [para. 326].

35. There is an oddity in assigning a grace with these meditations on the Three Kinds of Humility because the Three Kinds of Humility are not preceded by a specific prelude instructing us "to ask for what I want." Instead, the Three Kinds of Humility were given for meditation outside the normal five hours, and were meant to be pondered throughout the day. See Palmer, *On Giving the Spiritual Exercises*, 335, and see Fleming, *Draw Me into Your Friendship*, 126 [para. 164].

36. See Fleming, *Draw Me into Your Friendship*, 222 [para. 284].

37. See ibid., 224 [para. 285].

38. See ibid., 224 [para. 287].

39. See ibid., 218 [para. 277]. Although Ignatius used John 2:13–18, I am hoping to provide more continuity by staying with Matthew's text unless there is a particular advantage to refer to the Gospels of Luke or John.

40. See ibid., 224 [para. 286].

41. Ignatius called attention to both Peter and Judas in para. 289. See ibid., 226.

42. See ibid., 226 [para. 289]. Ignatius used John 13:21–30.

43. See ibid., 226 [para. 289].

44. See ibid., 132–44 [para. 169–89]. This is both very important and very complicated, and while this simplified method is a place to begin, I suggest a close reading of Gordon T. Smith's *Listening to God in Times of Choice: The Art of Discerning God's Will* (Downers Grove, IL: InterVarsity, 1997) as a helpful next step. Additionally one can look at his *The Voice of Jesus*, 128–56; and at Tad Dunne's *Spiritual Mentoring: Guiding People through Spiritual Exercises to Life Decisions* (San Francisco: HarperSanFrancisco, 1991).

The Third Movement

1. See Fleming, *Draw Me into Your Friendship*, 226 [para. 290]. In his Third Point, Ignatius referred to the bloodlike sweat in Luke 22:39–46. The first two points can be drawn from Matthew or Mark.

2. See ibid., 228 [para. 291].

3. See ibid., 228 [para. 292].

4. Tom Ashbrook, director of spiritual formation, Church Resource Ministries, identifies this as a serious failure among leaders in Protestant congregations worldwide in an email to me dated August 6, 2005.

5. See Fleming, *Draw Me into Your Friendship*, 230 [para. 293–95].

6. See ibid., 232 [para. 296]. Ignatius suggested we pray here with the account of the crucifixion found in John 19.

7. See ibid., 232 [para. 297].

8. See ibid., 232 [para. 298]. Ignatius includes Nicodemus as a witness to the burial, and so he had John 19 in mind again.

The Fourth Movement

1. Gerald G. May put it this way: "struggling with the very existence of self-image in the face of close appreciation of the divine." In *Care of Mind, Care of Spirit: Psychiatric Dimensions of Spiritual Direction* (San Francisco: Harper & Row, 1982), 47–48, 75.

2. See Fleming, *Draw Me into Your Friendship*, 176 [para. 234]. I have only slightly rephrased this to avoid the more archaic "Thee," "Thou," "Thy," and "Thine."

3. See ibid., 38 [para. 43].

4. See ibid., 258 [para. 327]. This is significantly rephrased.

Ignatian Resources

1. Father Mullan's translation was originally published as *The Spiritual Exercises of St. Ignatius* in New York in 1914. The literal translation was republished in David L. Fleming, S.J., *The Spiritual Exercises of St. Ignatius: A Literal Translation and*

Contemporary Reading (St. Louis: Institute of Jesuit Sources, 1978) and revised as *Draw Me into Your Friendship: A Literal Translation and a Contemporary Reading of The Spiritual Exercises* (St. Louis: Institute of Jesuit Sources, 1996). My use and paraphrase of the literal translation here is with the permission of John W. Padberg, S.J., director of the Institute of Jesuit Sources, and granted by letter on April 12, 2005.

2. See Fleming, *Draw Me into Your Friendship*, 26 [para. 23]. My rephrasing of the first sentence is supported by English, *Spiritual Freedom*, 19–25, esp. 295.

3. See Fleming, *Draw Me into Your Friendship*, 82–86 [para. 91–97]. I have only slightly rephrased the heart of these invitations as found in Part One, the Second Point [para. 93] and Part Two, the First Point [para. 95]. The positive responses anticipated in [para. 94] and [para. 96] are called for within the accompanying scriptural meditations. My rephrasing in Part One of "to conquer all the lands of unbelievers" as "to rid all lands of injustice and bring them real peace" is encouraged by both Fleming's paraphrase, and by English, *Spiritual Freedom*, 97.

4. This is significantly rephrased. See Fleming, *Draw Me into Your Friendship*, 116–20 [para. 149–57].

5. These are significantly rephrased to avoid the language of mortal and venial sins. See ibid., 128–30 [para. 165–68].

SACRED LISTENING
GLOSSARY

S OME PROTESTANTS MAY be unaccustomed to, or even uncomfortable with, terminology used in these Exercises. The following list will help familiarize you with the terms used in the instructions and throughout *Sacred Listening*. Additional definitions or explanations are covered as each is discussed.

consolation—a technical term defined at length in the third Rule for Discernment. Briefly, it is our experience of being called deeper into a relationship with God.

contemplate—to be in wonder with God and the text of Scripture. It is the fourth, and necessarily unfinished act in the *lectio divina*. We are called to live in contemplation.

desolation—a technical term defined at length in the fourth Rule for Discernment. Briefly, it is our experience of mistrusting God.

disciple—the person who makes the Exercises, commonly called the directee in writings on spiritual direction

grace, the—a gift of understanding, experience, and deep emotion we seek from God

Ignatian Parables—four meditative assignments that are introduced in the second movement

indifference, to find—seek to understand the value of all things as they serve the kingdom of God. Indifference is not a lack of passion or desire, it is a correct ordering of our desires relative to choosing the greater glory of the kingdom of God.

lectio divina—the art of sacred reading, comprised of four parts and described in more detail in chapter 2

listener—the person who listens to the disciples' review weekly

make (the Exercises), to—to do (the Exercises), and explained at length in chapter 2

meditate—literally, "to chew"; to prayerfully reflect on, it is also the second act in the *lectio divina*

repetition—to repeat for purposes of contemplating deeper meaning

Rules for Discernment (also called the Rules for Discerning Spirits)—an intuitive set of rules for understanding our experiences and emotional responses to them. Some describe our experience, while others counsel us on the best course of action.

spiritual director—one who is qualified to guide, mature in the faith and familiar with the Exercises

theme, the—the topic or focus of a unit

third listener—God is our first listener as we pray. We review with a human (second) listener. In teams of three, the third person listens to God and the review process as he or she prays for the disciple or human listener.

witness/witnessing—to enter into the Scripture reading as if we are there

Bibliography and
Suggestions for
Further Reading

T HE BIBLIOGRAPHY ON the *Spiritual Exercises* of Ignatius Loyola and on spiritual formation is immense. A comprehensive bibliography is not possible, and yet the author has found many of the following books and articles useful. Translations of the *Spiritual Exercises* are listed by the translator's last name. I have included the initials "S.J." to help readers identify works by Jesuit authors. I beg forgiveness where I have not been able to list this with complete accuracy.

Of all the works available on Ignatius's life and teachings, I recommend people begin with his autobiography. I prefer Tylenda's notations and comments. Olin also provides much useful information:

Tylenda, Joseph N., S.J., trans. *A Pilgrim's Journey: The Autobiography of Ignatius of Loyola*. Wilmington, DE: Michael Glazier, 1985.

Olin, John C., ed. *The Autobiography of St. Ignatius Loyola*. Translated by Joseph F. O'Callaghan. New York: Fordham, 1974, 1992.

Adams, Peter. *Hearing God's Words: Exporing Biblical Spirituality*. Vol. 16, *New Studies in Biblical Theology*. Downers Grove, IL: InterVarsity, 2004.

Allender, Dan B., and Tremper Longman. *The Cry of the Soul: How Our Emotions Reveal Our Deepest Questions About God*. Colorado Springs: NavPress, 1994.

Bakke, Jeannette A. *Holy Invitations: Exploring Spiritual Direction*. Grand Rapids: Baker, 2000.

Barry, William A., S.J. *Finding God in All Things: A Companion to The Spiritual Exercises of St. Ignatius*. Notre Dame, IN: Ave Maria Press, 1991.

———. *Letting God Come Close: An Approach to the Ignatian Spiritual Exercises*. Chicago: Loyola Press, 2001.

Barry, William A., S.J., and William J. Connolly, S.J. *The Practice of Spiritual Direction*. Minneapolis: Seabury Press, 1982.

Boyd, Gregory A. *Seeing Is Believing: Experiencing Jesus through Imaginative Prayer*. Grand Rapids: Baker, 2004.

Collins, Gary R. *The Magnificent Mind*. Waco: Word, 1985.

Conroy, Maureen. *The Discerning Heart: Discovering a Personal God*. Chicago: Loyola Press, 1993.

———. *Looking into the Well: Supervision of Spiritual Directors*. Foreword by George Aschenbrenner. Chicago: Loyola Press, 1995.

Cusson, Gilles, S.J. *Spiritual Exercises Made in Everyday Life: A Method and a Biblical Interpretation.* St. Louis: Institute of Jesuit Sources, 1989.

Dalmases, Cándido de. *Ignatius Loyola, Founder of the Jesuits: His Life and Work.* Translated by Jerome Aixalá. St. Louis: Institute of Jesuit Sources, 1985.

Dunne, Tad. *Spiritual Exercises for Today: A Contemporary Presentation of the Classic Spiritual Exercises of Ignatius Loyola.* San Francisco: HarperSanFrancisco, 1991.

———. *Spiritual Mentoring: Guiding People through Spiritual Exercises to Life Decisions.* San Francisco: HarperSanFrancisco, 1991.

Dyckman, Katherine, Mary Garvin, and Elizabeth Liebert. *The Spiritual Exercises Reclaimed: Uncovering Liberating Possibilities for Women.* New York/ Mahwah, NJ: Paulist Press, 2001.

Edwards, Tilden H. *Living in the Presence: Spiritual Exercises to Open Your Life to an Awareness of God.* San Francisco: HarperSanFrancisco, 1987, 1995.

———. *Spiritual Director, Spiritual Companion: Guide to Tending the Soul.* Mahwah, NJ: Paulist Press, 2001.

———. *Spiritual Friend.* New York: Paulist Press, 1980.

English, John J., S.J. *Spiritual Freedom: From an Experience of the Ignatian Exercises to the Art of Spiritual Guidance.* 2nd ed. Chicago: Loyola Press, 1995.

Fitzmyer, Joseph A., S.J. *Spiritual Exercises Based on Paul's Epistle to the Romans.* Grand Rapids: Eerdmans, 1995.

Fleming, David L., S.J. *Like the Lightning: The Dynamics of the Ignatian Exercises.* St. Louis: Institute of Jesuit Sources, 2004.

———. ed. *Notes on the Spiritual Exercises of St. Ignatius of Loyola.* St. Louis: Review for Religious, 1983.

———. *The Spiritual Exercises of St. Ignatius: A Literal Translation and Contemporary Reading.* St. Louis: Institute of Jesuit Sources, 1978. Revised as *Draw Me into Your Friendship: A Literal Translation and a Contemporary Reading of The Spiritual Exercises.* St. Louis: Institute of Jesuit Sources, 1996.

Foster, Richard J. *The Freedom of Simplicity.* San Francisco: Harper & Row, 1981.

Fowler, James W. *Faith Development and Pastoral Care.* Philadelphia: Fortress Press, 1987.

Ganss, George E., S.J. *The Spiritual Exercises of St. Ignatius: A Translation and Commentary.* Chicago: Loyola Press, 1992.

———. ed. *Ignatius of Loyola: Spiritual Exercises and Selected Works.* Classics of Western Spirituality. Ramsey, NJ: Paulist Press, 1991.

Green, Thomas H., S.J. *The Friend of the Bridegroom: Spiritual Direction and the Encounter with Christ.* Notre Dame, IN: Ave Maria Press, 2000.

———. *Prayer and Common Sense.* Notre Dame, IN: Ave Maria Press, 1995.

———. *A Vacation with the Lord.* Rev. ed. San Francisco: Ignatius Press, 2000.

———. *Weeds among the Wheat.* Notre Dame, IN: Ave Maria Press, 1984.

Guenther, Margaret. *Holy Listening: The Art of Spiritual Direction.* Cambridge, MA: Cowley Publications, 1992.

Hart, Thomas A. *The Art of Christian Listening.* Ramsey, NJ: Paulist Press, 1980.

Howard, Evan B. *Praying the Scriptures: A Field Guide for Your Spiritual Journey.* Downers Grove, IL: InterVarsity, 1999.

Hughes, Gerard W., S.J. *God of Surprises.* New York: Paulist Press, 1985.

Idígoras, J. Ignacio Tellechea. *Ignatius of Loyola: The Pilgrim Saint.* Translated and edited with preface by Michael Buckley, S.J. Chicago: Loyola University Press, 1994.

Lonsdale, David. *Eyes to See, Ears to Hear: An Introduction to Ignatian Spirituality. Traditions of Christian Spirituality.* Rev. ed. Maryknoll, NY: Orbis Books, 2000.

MacDonald, Gordon. "Mapping Your Private World: Journaling: A Tool to Bring Your Soul into Focus." *Leadership Journal* 25, no. 3 (2004): 88ff.

——. *Ordering Your Private World.* Nashville: Thomas Nelson, 1985.

May, Gerald G. *Care of Mind, Care of Spirit: Psychiatric Dimensions of Spiritual Direction.* San Francisco: Harper & Row, 1982.

Mottola, Anthony. *The Spiritual Exercises of St. Ignatius.* Introduction by Robert W. Gleason, S.J. New York: Doubleday, 1964.

Mueller, Joan. *Faithful Listening: Discernment in Everyday Life.* Kansas City, MO: Sheed & Ward, 1996.

Nemeck, Francis Kelly, and Marie Theresa Coombs. *The Way of Spiritual Direction.* Wilmington, DE: Michael Glazier, 1985.

O'Malley, John W., S.J. *The First Jesuits.* Cambridge, MA: Harvard, 1993.

Packer, James I. *Keep in Step with the Spirit.* Old Tappan, NJ: Revell, 1984.

Palmer, Martin E., S.J., trans. and ed. *On Giving the Spiritual Exercises: The Early Jesuit Manuscript Directories and the Official Directory of 1599.* St. Louis: Institute of Jesuit Sources, 1996.

Peterson, Eugene. *Christ Plays in Ten Thousand Places: A Conversation in Spiritual Theology.* Grand Rapids: Eerdmans, 2005.

——. *Eat This Book: A Conversation in the Art of Spiritual Reading.* Grand Rapids: Eerdmans, 2006.

——. *Reversed Thunder: The Revelation of John and the Praying Imagination.* San Francisco: Harper & Row, 1988.

——. "The Summer of My Discontent." *Christianity Today,* January 15, 1990, 28–30.

Puhl, Louis J., S.J. *The Spiritual Exercises of St. Ignatius: Based on Studies in the Language of the Autograph.* Chicago: Loyola Press, 1951. Originally published by Neuman Press.

Skehan, James W., S.J. *Director's Guide to Place Me with Your Son: Ignatian Spirituality in Everyday Life.* Washington, DC: Georgetown University Press, 1994.

——. *Place Me with Your Son: Ignatian Spirituality in Everyday Life.* 3rd ed. Washington, DC: Georgetown University Press, 1991.

Smith, Gordon T. *Listening to God in Times of Choice: The Art of Discerning God's Will.* Downers Grove, IL: InterVarsity, 1997.

——. *The Voice of Jesus: Discernment, Prayer, and the Witness of the Spirit.* Downers Grove, IL: InterVarsity, 2003.

Stanley, David M., S.J. *"I Encountered God!" The Spiritual Exercises with the Gospel of John.* St. Louis: Institute of Jesuit Sources, 1986.

Tetlow, Joseph, S.J. *Choosing Christ in the World: Directing the Spiritual Exercises of St. Ignatius Loyola according to Annotations Eighteen and Nineteen.* St. Louis: Institute of Jesuit Sources, 1989.

Toner, Jules J., S.J. *A Commentary on Saint Ignatius' Rules for the Discernment of Spirits.* St. Louis: Institute of Jesuit Sources, 1982.

———. *Discerning God's Will: Ignatius of Loyola's Teaching on Christian Decision Making*. St. Louis: Institute of Jesuit Sources, 1991.

———. *Spirit of Light or Darkness? A Casebook for Studying Discernment of Spirits*. St. Louis: Institute of Jesuit Sources, 1995.

Veltri, John A., S.J. *Orientations*. Vol. 1. Guelph, Ontario, Canada: Loyola House, 1979. Expanded and revised as *Orientations, Volume I: A Collection of Helps for Prayer*. Guelph, ON: Guelph Centre of Spirituality, 1993, 1996.

———. *Orientations*. Vol. 2. Guelph, ON: Loyola House, 1981. This was greatly expanded as *Orientations, Volume II: Part A: For Those Who Accompany Others on the Inward Journey*. Guelph, ON: Guelph Centre of Spirituality, 1998; and *Orientations, Volume II: Part B*. Guelph, ON: Guelph Centre of Spirituality, 1998.

Wiersbe, Warren W. *Preaching and Teaching with Imagination: The Quest for Biblical Ministry*. Grand Rapids: Baker, 1994.

Willard, Dallas. *The Divine Conspiracy: Rediscovering Our Hidden Life with God*. San Francisco: HarperSanFrancisco, 1998.

———. *In Search of Guidance*. Ventura, CA: Regal, 1984. Reprinted as *Hearing God: Developing a Conversational Relationship with God*. Downers Grove, IL: InterVarsity, 1999.

———. *Renovation of the Heart: Putting on the Character of Christ*. Colorado Springs: NavPress, 2002.

Wolff, Pierre, *Discernment: The Art of Choosing Well: Based on Ignatian Spirituality*. Rev. ed. Liguori, MO: Liguori Publications, 2003.

———. et al., trans. *The Spiritual Exercises of Saint Ignatius: A New Translation from the Authorized Latin Text*. Triumph Classic. Liguori, MO: Liguori Publications, 1997.

James L. Wakefield (M.Div., Denver Seminary; M.Th., Bethel Seminary; Ph.D., Marquette University) is associate professor of biblical and spiritual theology at Salt Lake Theological Seminary in Salt Lake City, Utah. He is associate pastor at Good Shepherd Lutheran Church in Sandy, Utah, and the author of *Jürgen Moltmann: A Research Bibliography*.

Please email comments and questions to: JLW1976@ alumni.usc.edu.